The Parent's Guide to

Family-Friendly Work

The Parent's Guide to

Family-Friendly Work

Finding the Balance Between Employment and Enjoyment

By Lori K. Long, Ph.D.

CAREER PRESS   The Career Press, Inc.
Franklin Lakes, N.J.

THE PARENT'S GUIDE TO FAMILY-FRIENDLY WORK
EDITED AND TYPESET BY GINA TALUCCI
Cover design by Jim Fanzone/Design Concepts
Printed in the U.S.A. by Book-mart Press

To order this title, please call toll-free 1-800-CAREER-1 (NJ and Canada: 201-848-0310) to order using VISA or MasterCard, or for further information on books from Career Press.

CAREER
PRESS

The Career Press, Inc., 3 Tice Road, PO Box 687,
Franklin Lakes, NJ 07417
www.careerpress.com

Library of Congress Cataloging-in-Publication Data

Long, Lori K., 1969-
    The Parent's guide to family-friendly work : finding the balance between employment and enjoyment / by Lori K. Long.
        p. cm.
    Includes index.
    ISBN-13: 978-156414-944-2
    ISBN-10: 1-56414-944-7
        1. Work and family—United States—Handbooks, manuals, etc. I. Title.

HD4904.25L66 2007
650.1--dc22

                                                            2007004925

To my family: David, Henry, and Emerson.

Acknowledgments

First, thanks to the staff at The Career Press for giving me the opportunity to publish this book. Thank you to all of my friends, colleagues, and family members who encouraged me to write this and helped me assemble the resources seen throughout the book. There are too many of you to list, and I would forget someone if I tried to do so. Thank you also to all of the parents who enthusiastically shared their stories with me.

Working parents raised me, and I never appreciated how hard the balancing act was for them. Thanks to my mom, Carol Welch, who instilled in me a love for books that led me to want to be an author. And to my dad, Jerry Kokensparger, who taught me how to work hard, providing me with the drive and discipline I needed to finish the book.

Finally, thank you most to my husband, David, and my kids, Henry and Emerson. My desire to find more time for them inspired me to create my own family-friendly work.

Contents

Introduction

Many working parents woke up today to sick children or a snowstorms that canceled school, and they struggled to figure out how to take care of their children and still make it to work. Some parents spent time today thinking about the next school year, trying to figure out how they can move ahead in their careers and still make sure their kids have somewhere to go after school. A few parents felt guilty today for not spending enough time with their kids and considered quitting their jobs.

Academic researchers have only just started exploring work and family conflict, leaving few answers for businesses and parents. Public policy and practice needs to change so that social supports exist to help us manage the challenge of working while raising a family. In the workplace, most research supports the idea that happier, more balanced workers have higher levels of productivity. When an employee feels a company supports him or her, the employee will likely stay longer with the company. Yet, many companies still do not have flexible work practices.

I sit in a coffee shop as I write today, in between dropping off and picking up kids from preschool. As I look around the coffee shop, I see that I am not the only one working. Two men and one other woman sit poised behind laptops sipping coffee. One wears jeans, comfortable clothes similar to me. The others look they may be going into an office, or to meet clients later. A group of women seem engaged in a meeting; one brings a small child with her. These scenes remind me that the nature of work has changed. Technology and changing company policies allow more and more people to enjoy flexibility in their work. Flexibility means having some control over when, where, and how much you work.

I didn't really know what family-friendly meant to me until I had children and started to experience some challenges. I had my first child while in graduate school. At the time, I was teaching, doing research, and consulting work for small businesses. While I worked many hours each week, I mostly set my own schedule. I had to show up for the classes I taught, but could prepare for class or grade papers at any time I chose (such as well after midnight while the baby slept). I realized very quickly that my flexible work arrangement would allow me to meet many parenting challenges.

When my son stayed home sick, I appreciated the fact that I could easily stay home with him and work while he napped. Later, when preschool held the big "Muffins with Mom" party at 10 a.m. on a Wednesday morning, I was thrilled I could attend. The realization of my good fortune in finding a flexible arrangement crystallized further as I witnessed other parents deciding to give up their careers, if only for a while, because they could not create a flexible enough arrangement for their own needs. Many did this because they did not know family-friendly work exists, or at least how to find it.

I believe we can change the flexible work practices in the work world one company at a time. By demanding flexibility to meet your family needs, you may be able to demonstrate to just one company the return of such practices. As more companies uncover the payback in increased employee commitment and productivity, flexible work options will become the norm. But, in order to demand flexibility, you must first understand it. You need to know what to ask for and how to ask for it. You may also need to leave your current company to find a family-friendly opportunity. Further, family-friendly work may require other paths, such as working on your own, or staying home for a while.

About Me

Throughout this book, I will share my own work and family experiences. Many friends have told me that they would prefer to have an arrangement similar to mine. I spend as much time as I want with my kids, and have a fulfilling career. My work and family arrangement is a little disjointed and often confusing, so I would like to share my background with you.

After graduating from college and working a little while in sales, I decided to switch gears and pursue a career in human resource management (HR). After several years in the field, I made the choice to pursue an academic career. I started working as the associate director of a career center in a business school, finding my HR experience valuable in coaching graduates in career planning. But after a couple of years, I decided that administration wasn't for me.

So I moved on to graduate school (again) and started working on my Ph.D. I planned to get my degree, and then search nationwide for a college teaching opportunity. But with more than five years of work on my degree, I had two children, my husband had become a partner at his accounting firm, and we moved into a house in a community in which we wanted to raise our children. So instead of relocating, I started an HR consulting company and started teaching part-time at a small local college. Someday, I would like to teach full-time, but for now, my work arrangement works for me.

I have very flexible work. I often teach at night, and much of my teaching-related work can be done in the evenings or while the kids nap. I can also take on or turn down as much consulting work as I choose. Typically, I take my kids to Laura (the childcare provider who you will hear more about) two or three days a week, leaving me at least a couple of days at home with the kids. I really enjoy both of my worlds immensely, and feel very fortunate to have such a situation.

I also have a spouse with whom I can share some flexible joint parenting. As a partner at a CPA firm, Dave has some control over his schedule, and he works in a business where he has some flexibility. He can go in late if necessary, but he also might have to take a client out to dinner in the evening.

Because of my personal opportunity to create a family-friendly work arrangement, along with my professional experience in career counseling and human resource management, I am in a unique position to offer you some specific advice about finding family-friendly work that benefits you; I know you will succeed.

How to Use This Book

Unfortunately, no step-by-step formula exists to create the ultimate family-friendly work arrangement. This book is a collection of ideas and resources. Therefore, you may or may not need to read every chapter in this book. If you have no idea what you want to do, then read it all. I hope that you hold on to this book, and refer to it regularly as your needs change, because they will!

Part

1

Planning
Your
Future

Chapter

1

What You Weren't Told About "Having It All"

Do you remember what you wanted to be when you grew up? I recall several years in my preteens focusing on my future career as a teacher. As I entered high school, my thoughts turned to more business-like pursuits, such as marketing or advertising. By the time I started college, I had changed my mind again, and I continued to change my mind and make plans all the way through my 20s. I went to graduate school, twice. Similar to many people, I twisted and turned through my career path, spending much time reflecting on finding a meaningful career choice.

Not once during all of my planning and preparing did I consider where parenthood would fit in my career. I knew someday I would be a parent, but I just didn't consider how it would affect my career plans. I never imagined that I would face the difficult decisions about work that I did once I had children. Would I continue to work? If so, how could I create a work situation that fulfilled me while meeting the needs of my children?

You can "have it all." At least that's what I was told. Growing up, teachers asked about career interests. Our high school counselors signed us up for college preparatory courses, and told us we could do whatever we wanted with our lives. No one asked about plans to have a family. After all, in today's world anyone who works hard can have a successful career, an adoring spouse, and happy kids all in a two-story house in the suburbs with a white picket fence.

But if you have started your career, married that perfect spouse, and had those kids, you know that having it all isn't quite so easy. Pursuing your career becomes a tough path if it means giving up time with your kids. And if you spend time with your kids and work, you are most likely not living in that perfectly kept house or spending much time with that adoring spouse.

Work and Family As Opposing Forces

Once you have children, time becomes more valuable, because you want to spend more time with them. However, time becomes the enemy when trying to balance work and family. You want to spend time at work because you enjoy what you do, or you need to earn more money or the next promotion. You also want to spend time with your children, to take care of their needs and to love and enjoy them.

In addition to your time, you face a conflict with your attention and energy as well. You need to focus on your work, but problems at home can make that a challenge. For example, you can't concentrate on your work if you don't feel comfortable about your childcare arrangements. Further, your work often invades your home life, especially as technology has made it so easy to check messages or speak to a coworker from anywhere. As a deadline looms, you may find yourself working at home instead of spending the time you want with your children.

Children's needs also do not come with a reliable schedule. In fact, they tend to need things at the most inopportune times. It never fails: I have a training program scheduled with hundreds of attendees on the same day my husband has a meeting with a potential new client—and a child wakes up sick. Even if your kids stick to a schedule, the schedule tends to change often. One season may be soccer and the next season ballet. School schedules change almost yearly. If you find a work-and-family arrangement that works for you, it will only be a temporary solution because things will change.

Finally, finances work against you in your work and family decisions. Adding children to your home significantly increases your need for income. You now have another person for whom you need to provide, clothe, and feed. If you choose to work, childcare expenses can take away a large chunk of your salary. At a time when you think you may need to cut back at work, you face an exponential increase in your expenses.

Some challenges for women

Have you ever seen a "Working Father" magazine? Men do not always have the same stress in balancing work and family that women face. Women tend to take on more domestic responsibility at home. If you have children, you most likely take on most of the coordinating, record keeping, and other primary care responsibilities. Further, many women often strive for perfection, creating more stress then necessary. I know my husband would take on more if I asked (never mind that I have to ask), but I have difficulty letting some things go. For example, I pick out the children's clothes in the morning because I do not want my 2-year-old daughter heading out in the world wearing a blue sweatshirt paired with purple plaid velvet pants.

Further, women often face more opposition in the workplace when trying to manage family responsibilities. Men often receive accolades in the workplace when they need to do things for their families. My husband tells me how the women in his office comment on his family dedication when he leaves work to take care of the kids when I have to teach, or when he works from home due to a sick kid. Women, however, often don't mention family obligations in fear of being labeled as uncommitted to their careers.

Therefore, women committed to their careers often face a significant challenge in creating a family-friendly work arrangement. If you take on more home responsibilities, you will need to adjust your schedule at work. But, if you seek out an alternate work schedule, you may be viewed as uncommitted in a work sense.

Some challenges for men

While men are often revered in the workplace when they take on more responsibility at home, they still face challenges. Men do not share their frustrations with each other the way women do. Working mothers tend to seek each other out and provide guidance and support. However, working fathers do not readily open up to each other to talk about work and family challenges. Often working fathers feel isolated.

Many men choose to stay home with kids or take on a part-time role simply because they want to. Sometimes, however, they make this choice because their wife makes more money in her career. Some men facing this option find it troubling. While they look forward to more involvement with their children's lives, they may face some ego challenges in taking the backseat on the career path.

Finally, many men perceive family-friendly policies, such as flexible work, as benefits for women, and they fear they will face penalties for taking advantage of such benefits. Men face a stigma attached to working in an alternate work arrangement or taking advantage of family-friendly benefits. One working father shared with me that his boss suggested he note his time off after the birth of his first child simply as vacation time instead of family leave, so that "no one would get the wrong idea" about his commitment to the company.

The challenge as parents

Not only do you face challenges in deciding how you want to manage your career, but you must also consider your spouse's career plans as well. Finding a family-friendly work arrangement must include involving your spouse in your plans to make sure your children and your home receive the care they need.

If both parents have strong career aspirations, the decision on how to manage children becomes even more complex. If the arrangement causes one parent to take on a different role than the other, feelings of resentment may arise. If you choose to stay at home more with the kids, you may feel resentful toward your spouse for moving ahead more rapidly with his or her career. Or if you choose to focus more on your career while your spouse has the flexibility to spend more time with the kids, you may feel resentment toward your spouse for getting time with the kids that you do not.

How to "Have It All"

Before you begin to consider a family-friendly work arrangement, you must decide what "having it all" means to you. First, you may want to consider rethinking your definition of success. Early in my career, I thought success meant climbing to the top of the ladder that stood before me; I'm now building my own ladder. I've decided that success, for me, means that I have meaningful work, a steady income, and a happy family.

Instead of trying to keep your work from invading your family and your family from invading your work, consider ways to integrate your work and your life. Start working on getting an arrangement that allows you to do both without neglecting either. Undoubtedly, if you have a family, regardless of what you see as success, a family-friendly work arrangement will benefit you.

Your definition of "family-friendly" most likely differs from mine. A family-friendly work situation depends on what your family needs. Everyone raises children under different circumstances and constraints. Further, the support of others has a significant impact on your workplace needs for flexibility. For example, your spouse may work many extra hours each week providing you with little or no assistance. Alternatively, you could be a single parent with no immediate family around to help you. Parents in both of these situations have far different needs than parents with spouses who work reasonable hours with some flexibility. Further, parents with strong local networks of friends and family often can work in less flexible working arrangements than those without such a network.

The age and activities of your children will also affect your workplace needs. Your children may be young and completely dependent on you, or your children may be school-aged, involved in many activities, and need a taxi service. Your kids may need you to help them get on the bus in the morning, or your kids may need you after school to help with homework. But remember, your family needs will likely change as your children go through different stages in life.

Only you can determine your own family-friendly work needs. Ultimately, family-friendly work allows you to find balance between work that fulfills you personally, and a family that needs your time and attention.

Chapter Wrap-Up

You may already know the challenge you have ahead of you. You may be so wrapped up in your dilemma that you do not believe a solution exists. Let me assure you that a solution does exist. You can't change the needs your children have, but you can change the way you meet those needs. Finding or creating a family-friendly work arrangement will allow you to meet your children's needs, as well as your own. Face your challenges with your goal in sight. You can have a successful career and a family at the same time; it will just take some work to get the right arrangement in place.

Resources

Books for Women

Creating a Life: Professional Women and the Quest for Children by Sylvia Ann Hewlett (Talk Miramax Books, 2002).

Getting It Right: How Working Mothers Successfully Take Up the Challenge of Life, Family, and Career by Lorraine Zappert (Pocket Books, 2001).

Perfect Madness: Motherhood in the Age of Anxiety by Judith Warner (Riverhead Books, 2001).

The Price of Motherhood: Why the Most Important Job in the World is Still the Least Valued by Ann Crittenden (Henry Holt, 2001).

This Is How We Do It: The Working Mothers' Manifesto by Carol Evans (Hudson Street Press, 2006).

Books for Men

Father Courage: What Happens When Men Out Family First by Suzanne Braun Levine (Harcourt, 2000).

Working Fathers: New Strategies for Balancing Work and Family by James Levine and Todd Pittinsky (Harcourt Brace and Company, 1998).

Chapter

2

Preparing for Family-Friendly Work

Luck is where preparedness meets opportunity. I heard that on *Oprah* a while back. I don't often quote celebrities, but when I heard this, it stuck with me. Other parents often tell me that I am "lucky" to have my work arrangement. I have a fulfilling career, but I still spend as much time as I want with my kids. For the most part, I have solved the difficult equation that allows me to successfully integrate work into my life. I used to think I was "lucky," too. But then I heard Oprah Winfrey's definition of luck: Luck is where preparedness meets opportunity.

I have this great work/life arrangement because I had the right preparation when the right opportunities came my way. I knew what kind of work I wanted to do, and I had the skills I needed when I came across interesting work. I teach college courses because I have the right credentials. I am writing this book because I have the expertise needed to secure a book contract. I have a great childcare provider who allows me to work without worrying about my kids. I have a husband with some flexibility in his schedule, so he can back me up when we have a childcare problem.

However, you don't need my expertise and experience to get a family-friendly arrangement. The expertise you need depends on your profession and what you aspire to do. But I will tell you the more education and experience you have in your vocation, the more likely you can demand the work situation you want.

Three key steps prepare you to search for family-friendly work. First, you must identify your home and your career priorities, and create a plan to find an arrangement that supports your priorities. Next, you must get the resources in place to support your plan (Chapter 3), and finally, you may need to take steps to increase your expertise to help you realize your plan (Chapter 4). Further, as you develop your plan, you need to consider your current, as well as your future, situation.

Ideally, you should pursue a family-friendly work arrangement before your current work arrangement becomes unbearable. You must evaluate your situation, identify your priorities, and make a plan before you become desperate. Often, parents decide to make a change after things have become too difficult. If stress and exasperation guide your decision-making, you might move too rapidly toward any option, instead of the best option for you.

Know Your Priorities

As we learned in Chapter 1, rarely can you "have it all." While some parents seem to have it all together, reality leads us to do less. I've come to the realization that I can't have it all. But I do get the choice of what I don't have. For me, I've given up any domestic aspirations. Not that I've ever had a sparkling clean house, but I used to make an effort. Now, I will usually only clean up when we expect guests, and I occasionally hire someone to thoroughly clean. I also don't have creative scrapbooks, well-organized closets, or homemade meals every night. For the most part, I've put home-making on the back burner. Instead, I have a career that I find fulfilling and financially beneficial, and I have some quality time with my family.

Home priorities

You must first consider your priorities for your family and your home. When it comes to your children, you need to determine what you want for them. Do you want to spend more time with them and help them do their homework? Do you want to run them to activities? Or do you just need some flexibility to deal with unexpected events such as an illness? Many home factors may affect what kind of work arrangement to pursue. For example, Donna and Mark both wanted to pursue their careers, full force. But they also did not want their kids spending more time in childcare than in their own care. So,

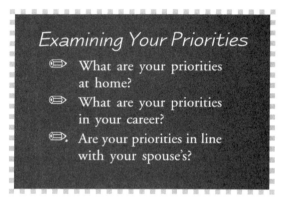

Examining Your Priorities

☞ What are your priorities at home?

☞ What are your priorities in your career?

☞ Are your priorities in line with your spouse's?

they decided to share the childcare responsibilities. Donna negotiated an arrangement to stay home two days each week. Mark, who was self-employed, stayed home one day each week, leaving the kids in daycare only two days each week.

Establishing your priorities also includes evaluating your financial situation. Whether you face the challenge of being a single parent, or you just want to achieve a certain lifestyle, you need to determine how much money you need to earn. Take some time to make a budget so you know exactly how you spend your money. Chapter 3 further discusses evaluating your financial resources. A clear understanding of your needed income will help you determine how much you need to work to support your family.

Consider your own, and your children's hobbies or activities. Do you belong to every organization you come across just because you think you should? You must carefully prioritize what organizations you belong to and at what level you wish to become involved with the organization. For example, I belong to my local PTA because it allows me to get to know my children's friends' parents. However, I try to find volunteer opportunities with the group that do not take too much of my time. I also belong to a couple of professional organizations because they help me stay networked (see Chapter 12) and up-to-date in my field (see Chapter 4).

You also need to be sure you evaluate your child's activities. My 4-year-old son has friends who play soccer, t-ball, take swimming lessons, music lessons, gymnastics, and on and on. Often, as parents, we feel pressure to do the same lest we become marked as uncaring parents. While I know many of these activities will enrich my son's development, my husband and I have decided that we want to focus on spending more time with our kids. I don't want our time together to just involve running from activity to activity. So we pick one activity at a time. Remember that your kids will often benefit just as much from an evening home playing games with the family as with an evening at the soccer field.

Even if you don't give up some domestic or other activities completely, consider lowering your involvement or standards. For example, if you can't give up vacuuming your house regularly, try once a week instead of once a day. If your child really wants to play soccer, try joining a league that meets once a week instead of a traveling league. My husband enjoys playing softball, but once we had kids, he switched from a league that played two nights a week to one that played one night a week. That extra free evening each week makes a huge difference in our family time.

Sit down and spend some time considering your priorities at home. Do you want to make changes? If so, where? Once you know your home priorities, you must next look at your career priorities.

Career priorities

You need to define your priorities when it comes to your work as well. Consider why you work. Do you need to work for financial support? Do you want to work for personal fulfillment? Do you just need some adult interaction? You must take some time to figure out what you want to do and why you want to do it.

Consider your short-term and your long-term career goals. When you consider your long-term plans, what do you need to accomplish in the short-term to meet your long-term goals? How do you feel about the progress of your career? Many parents mistakenly assume that they have to put career aspirations on hold in order to have a family-friendly work arrangement. Often, you can more easily establish a family-friendly arrangement through slowing down the progression of your career, but you do not have to. You can establish a work arrangement that gives you some flexibility to meet your family needs, and still progress in your career. You need to decide, however, if you want to dedicate yourself to that pursuit.

Ideally, you must enjoy your work to establish a truly family-friendly work arrangement. If you don't enjoy your work, you will only resent your job more, because it takes you away from your kids. If you love your current vocation, you have a head start in the process. If not, you will not necessarily be behind. Searching for a flexible work opportunity may also give you a chance to change careers. Complete career selection advice is beyond the scope of this book, but I've listed some excellent resources at the end of this chapter to help you find your career path. You must, however, invest some time to find the type of work that you will find fulfilling.

My friend Christy recently transitioned to a nonprofit career in arts management from the corporate world. She made this move after years of reflection and consideration. While she still works full-time, she has found more family-friendly work because she loves what she does. Her satisfaction with her new career reflects upon her daughter. She enjoys engaging her daughter in work-related activities, and now finds more work-life integration instead of work-life conflict.

In addition to understanding the type of work you want to pursue, you also need to determine what kind of work arrangement you want. Do you want part-time work, or just more flexibility? Chapters 8 and 9 lay out the various options to consider. If you already have kids, you can start considering what kind of work arrangement to pursue by considering what problems you have with your current arrangement. Look at what areas of your life cause you stress to determine what kind of arrangement might make sense for you.

You must consider your current, as well as your future needs. Ultimately, I would like to teach full-time at a college, so now I am taking steps to position myself for that pursuit. I currently teach part-time with a plan to go full-time after my kids start school. Right now, I could make more money if I did more consulting work instead of teaching, but the teaching helps me keep my foot in the door until I want to go full-time. In fact, some professions make it difficult to take time off and return to work later. An attorney, for example, will have much more difficulty returning to work if he or she does not keep his or her credentials up to date. Further, in many professions, the business changes quickly, and a few years out the loop will put you behind. For example, a graphic designer that does not stay up-to-date with the latest software might as well return to school to start over.

Coordinating your priorities as parents

If you have a partner in raising your children, your assessment of your home and career priorities should be a joint activity. A family-friendly work arrangement requires both parents to work together to find an arrangement that works. Avoid making assumptions as you make your plan. Do not assume it is the woman's role to handle the children. Also, do not assume that the higher wage earner should keep working full-time. Often, the most family-friendly arrangement may require the higher wage earner to have more flexibility. You will find what works best if you consider all of your options and challenge your assumptions.

Many parents hold strong beliefs about the care for their children, and insist on managing on their own without the help of an outside care provider. In these situations, parents often pursue what we refer to as a "split-shift" arrangement. Under this arrangement, parents work alternate shifts, such as one working the day shift and one working the evening shift. While such an arrangement does make childcare easier, you must remember that it makes marriage more difficult, and it creates challenges in maintaining a family life. Parents who make a decision for such an arrangement should dedicate some efforts to find time for each other, as well as for family activities.

Keys to Success

As you start your quest for family-friendly work, you must make sure you have the right mindset. First, you must assess your work style to make sure you will succeed in an alternate work arrangement. You must be patient in your pursuit, while forging forward with a positive outlook. You must also keep the future in mind.

Who succeeds in alternate work

Regardless of your priorities, family-friendly work will most likely require some kind of alternate work arrangement, such as part-time work or a flexible schedule option. Before deciding on an option to pursue, you must consider if you can succeed in an alternate work arrangement. Some find alternate work arrangements challenging, preferring more structure and stability. Also, you may be the lone employee with an alternate work arrangement at your company, so you must be comfortable doing something other than the norm. Further, certain types of flexible work arrangements may be more challenging for some. For example, if you pursue work that requires a great deal of autonomy, but you lack self-motivation, you will likely fail. To succeed in an alternate work arrangement you must:

➥ **Be confident in your career.** Pursuing anything other than a traditional path can be challenging. You must feel strongly that you can succeed.

➥ **Work well independently.** Often, an alternate work arrangement requires you to organize your own work. You must be able to accomplish this with little supervision.

➥ **Be highly motivated.** Working independently requires a high level of self-motivation.

➥ **Be a good communicator.** You will often have limited opportunities to meet and communicate with others. You must be effective in your communication to make the most of those limited opportunities.

➥ **Be organized and efficient.** If you must accomplish your work in a limited schedule, you must be able to organize your work so that you can succeed.

➥ **Be flexible.** If you expect flexibility from your company, you must also provide flexibility to your company.

Remember it takes time

If you could find a family-friendly work option with ease, you probably wouldn't be reading this book. Family-friendly work options are often hidden; the research and networking required to uncover such opportunities takes time. Also, family-friendly options often require further education or skills that take time to develop as well. You may be seeking a quick fix, assuming a book such as this will give you a simple step-by-step plan to find family-friendly work in a day. Unfortunately, a quick fix typically only provides a temporary solution. A valuable long-term successful work option requires planning and work to achieve.

You must take time to plan, so you do not rush into an arrangement that doesn't work for you. Hopping from job to job trying to find a good work arrangement will only hurt you by creating a history of instability that many companies will avoid. Further, you must continue to stay positive in your quest for family-friendly work. A positive outlook will help you approach your search with determination.

Your future plans

You will need to revisit your home and career priorities several times as your children grow up. You may find that as your children become teenagers, they require more of your time than they did as toddlers. Further, you need to consider how your current career plans affect your future career plans. For example, you may decide that you want to stay home for some time. If you do, you must consider both the long-term career and financial affects of this decision. Will you still be able to move forward in your career if you step away for a few years? How will the decision affect your long-term financial stability? If you have been out of the workforce for several years, you may be able to jump back in around the same place you left off, but you will not likely be able to have the same salary that you would have earned had you kept working. This decision also significantly affects your retirement savings.

After their first child was born, Kevin and Allison decided that it made sense for him to go part-time at the small company where he worked as a graphic designer. Allison was at a pivotal point in her career, and felt she needed to continue to work full-time. A few years and a few children later, comfortable with her advancement, they considered having Allison transition to part-time while Kevin returned to full-time. However, Kevin's part-time work slowed down his career progression, and he was unable to match the salary that Allison had earned working full-time. They both had to work full-time for a while to save enough money to make the transition.

A plan for you

When my son was six months old, I became suddenly ill. No one could figure out what was wrong with me, I just felt bad all of the time. I lost a significant amount of weight, and didn't feel like working, or doing anything at all. I finally figured out that I was suffering from anxiety. For me, the anxiety was caused by my hectic schedule and the unrealistic demands I was putting on myself. I had taken on more work than I could handle, and I was still trying to take time off to spend with my son.

Since then I have made it a priority to take care of myself first. I try to eat better, and I always make sure I get exercise. If your life only involves rushing to and from work and managing your kids, you will go nuts. You need to carve out some time for yourself. Whether you have a hobby, or just socialize with friends, you must have some "me" time.

I recently returned from an annual college reunion weekend with my girlfriends, Vanessa, Michelle, and Kathy. These trips rejuvenate me. Just laughing and talking about the old days reminds me of who I was before I had children. Finding that person among the mother/consultant/educator I am now helps keep me on track.

Chapter Wrap-Up

Before you can start searching for a family-friendly work arrangement, you must first know your priorities both at home and in your career. You can mitigate some of the guilt you might feel about leaving your children to go to work if you have deliberately planned a work situation that allows you to serve the family role that you want to serve. Once you have your plan in place, be prepared to change it often. Work changes, your kids needs change, and sometimes you just want something different. The more forward-thinking you are, the more easily you will meet future challenges.

Resources

Books

100 Ways to Motivate Yourself: Change Your Life Forever by Steve Chandler (Career Press, 2004).

Do What You Are: Discover the Perfect Career for You Through the Secrets of Personality Type by Paul D. Tieger and Barbara Barron-Tieger (Little, Brown and Company, 2001)

Do What You Love, The Money Will Follow: Discovering Your Right Livelihood by Marsha Sinetar (Dell, 1989).

I Could Do Anything If I Only Knew What It Was: How to Discover What You Really Want and How to Get It by Barbara Sher (Dell, 1995).

Just Kiss Me and Tell Me You Did the Laundry by Karen Bouris (Rodale, 2004).

What Color Is Your Parachute? 2007: A Practical Manual for Job-Hunters and Career-Changers by Richard Nelson Bolles (Ten Speed Press, 2006).

Write It Down Make It Happen: Knowing What You Want And Getting It by Henriette Anne Klauser (Touchstone, 2001).

Websites

The Career Key: *www.careerkey.org*
Online assessment tool to assist with identifying interests and career planning.

The Integrated Mother: *www.integratedmother.com*

The Integrated Mother is a nationwide coaching and training company that helps frazzled working moms who are struggling with the demands of career and motherhood.

Jobs and Moms Career Consulting: *www.jobsandmoms.com*
A Website for professional women looking for better ways to blend career and family. The site includes a flexible jobs board, an entrepreneurial zone, articles, a free newsletter, and dozens of other mom-friendly career-oriented resources.

Chapter 3

The Resources You Need

Our personal and family responsibilities often invade our work creating stress and conflict. The less you have to worry about your family while you work, the more you can concentrate, be productive, and increase your value to your company. If you do so, your company will more likely grant your request for a flexible work arrangement. Therefore, you must have the right resources and support in place to take care of your personal and familial needs.

If you try to do everything yourself, you will never create a work arrangement that allows you to balance your work with your family. There are just not enough hours in the day to do everything you want, or need to do to manage your family and work. Supporting resources can help make your work arrangement family-friendly.

> ### Resources You'll Need
>
> ➯ Your spouse and kids.
> ➯ Domestic help.
> ➯ Childcare.
> ➯ Other resources.

Your Partner and Your Kids

Insist that your spouse or partner take on an appropriate share of the domestic workload. Also, work with your spouse or partner to see what he or she can do to have more flexibility in his or her work. As outlined in Chapter 2, family-friendly work requires family support. If your spouse does not have flexibility with his or her work, determine what else you can do to fairly balance home and childcare responsibilities.

Enlist your kids to help out, too. Even if you have young children, they can contribute to housework. My toddlers know where their dirty clothes go and have to keep their own playroom clean. While the child's perspective on what constitutes a clean playroom differs a little from mine, they enjoy the responsibility. Unloading the dishwasher and folding laundry involve a team effort at my house. My 2-year-old does not have good towel folding skills, but we spend some quality time together working at it.

Domestic Services

By the time you take care of your work and your children, you may find little time or interest in taking care of things around your home. As you work out your financial situation, consider what home duties you can outsource. You can pick to

Domestic Services Outsourcing Ideas

- Housecleaning.
- Lawn service.
- Professional organizer.
- Food preparation.
- Online help.
- General errands.

outsource what you don't enjoy doing, or what you just can't find time to do.

Housecleaning

Consider hiring a cleaning service to clean your house on a regular basis. You don't have to have someone come in every week. I used to have a service come in just for special occasions, such as if we were entertaining, or if we had guests coming in from out of town. Since I started working on this book, I have less time each week, so now I have someone come in once a month. Not only do I have more time to work because I have less cleaning to do, the cleaners do a much better job than I ever have.

Lawn care

You can hire a landscaping service or just a neighborhood kid to cut your grass on a regular basis; or you may want to only have them come in once a month or so. You can also just get help seasonally. My brother Tod, whose second-grader tries to help with lawn work, also hires a teenager to help out with mulch spreading in the spring and raking in the fall.

Professional organizer

How many hours do you spend each month searching for a lost item in your house? If you can't seem to get organized and your life seems to always be in disarray, you may want to consider getting professional help. A professional organizer can help organize your home and even your office. You can save a lot of time around the house if you have your house organized to correspond with your activities and needs.

Food preparation service

Several Websites exist that help you make mealtime at home easier. You can enter your preferences and receive a custom menu for the week that includes a grocery list. This list can be customized to your local grocery store, so that you can work your way through the store without wasting time backtracking to get something you missed.

In addition to shopping assistance, another kind of food preparation help has surfaced that allows you to create "make and take" meals. These companies allow you to come in and spend a few hours creating meals that you can freeze and later cook in the crockpot, bake in the oven, or throw on the grill. All of the recipe ingredients are cleaned, chopped, and cut. You just measure and mix. You can offer your family good food with little effort on your part. Plus, you can go with your spouse or a group of friends to prepare the dinners, making a fun night out.

Online help

You can save a significant amount of time shopping and taking care of other business using the Internet. You can arrange to pay all of your bills without taking the time to write out checks, prepare envelopes, and mail. You can take care of your shopping needs from buying gifts and toys, to groceries and paper products. You can often find online shopping prices lower than similar in-store products, and many online retailers offer shipping discounts. I buy everything from diapers to books online and save myself hours because I don't have to drive to the store and walk around searching for things. Even better, I can shop without strapping my toddlers into car seats and trying to keep them entertained in a store.

General errands

Some entrepreneurs have figured out that busy working parents need help running errands. These businesses often advertise themselves as concierge or just an errand-running service. Such businesses offer a wide variety of services, generally the things you don't have time for, such as taking your car to the mechanic, doing your grocery shopping, or picking up your dry-cleaning. Often, the time you save by having someone help you with daily errands can make the cost of these services more than worthwhile.

Childcare

Your childcare needs depend on the age of your children. Parents of babies and toddlers find childcare challenging, but sometimes forget that the concern does not end when kids start school. Many schools only offer half-day kindergarten classes. Further, most school schedules do not coincide with traditional work schedules. Your child might get off the bus at 3:30 p.m. while you work until 5 p.m. And then summer comes and you have a few full months of childcare to figure out.

Think creatively about childcare options. What do you really need? If you plan to work part-time or a flexible

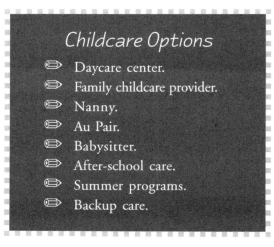

Childcare Options

➯ Daycare center.
➯ Family childcare provider.
➯ Nanny.
➯ Au Pair.
➯ Babysitter.
➯ After-school care.
➯ Summer programs.
➯ Backup care.

schedule, finding childcare will actually be a little more difficult. Many daycare centers do not have part-time options. Or if they do, you must lock-in on certain days. I had this difficulty when I was looking for childcare. One center had a part-time opening, but could only do a Monday, Wednesday, and Friday schedule. Because of teaching, my schedule changes every few months so this wouldn't work. Instead, I found a family childcare provider who liked my flexibility.

Whatever option you choose, make sure you dedicate some time to thoroughly checking out the center or person you select. Often, local reports exist that give you information on area daycare centers. Check in with your state family services office, or a local librarian to find resources in your area. If you go with an individual provider such as a family childcare provider, nanny, or babysitter, you should also do a thorough investigation. You can hire a background check agency, or find an online service that provides background reports. You should check references, verify education and past employment history, search criminal records, and also driving records if the individual will drive your children.

Daycare center

Many working parents find a daycare center to be the best option. Daycare centers typically open early and close late each day. They rarely close, except for holidays. They can offer your child some stability, as a daycare center will most likely be available for the span of your child's life.

You must select a daycare center carefully. Just because a daycare center has a license to operate does not mean that it provides the quality care you need. Some daycare centers have few structured activities and suffer from a high turnover of caregivers. If your child does not adapt well to change, a revolving door of caregivers can add unnecessary trauma to his or her life.

Family childcare provider

A family childcare provider cares for your children in his or her own home. We chose a family childcare arrangement because it offered the flexibility that we needed. My son started with Nicole who took care of her two children, my son, and three other toddlers. We moved when my son was a year old and found Laura, who has now taken care of our kids for more than three years. The kids love to go, starting almost every morning with the question, "Are we going to Miss Laura's today?" I think our situation works well because I have the flexibility to work around Laura's needs, as much as she has the flexibility to work around my needs. Every season we set a schedule, and then deviate from it often. We communicate via e-mail on a weekly basis to confirm any schedule changes.

If you don't have much flexibility, a family childcare provider might create some challenges. For example, if Laura's kids are home sick, I have to find another option for my kids. Or when one of Laura's family needs conflict with some of my work needs, we also need to adjust our schedule and possibly use backup care.

We were fortunate to find Laura, who takes great care of our kids. Some family childcare providers don't offer the same quality that a daycare center provides. If the caregiver has too many children or does not engage the children in activities, it could be a worrisome experience. Make sure you ask the provider about nap accommodations and what kind of activities he or she provides for the children.

Nanny

A nanny is a professional childcare provider that may live in your home, or just come to your home on a daily basis. A nanny sometimes will also take care of some domestic responsibilities, but usually only those related to the children. Megan, who has her own dental practice, has found a nanny makes her less stressed about the care of her two young boys because she has more flexibility. She also finds more time because her nanny comes to her home, so she does not have to rush out of the house each day. This custom care creates the perfect solution for many families, however, a nanny will often be much more costly than other care options.

Au pair

An au pair is a foreign national student that comes to the United States as an exchange student and lives with a host family. In exchange for room and board and a stipend, the au pair provides childcare service. Colette believes an au pair is a great option for her family. The young lady living with them has exposed her young children to a new language and new cultural experiences. In addition, the live-in help gives her the flexibility she needs.

Babysitter

You may be able to cover your childcare needs by simply using a babysitter. For example, if you choose to work part-time from home, you may just need someone a few hours a day to care for your kids while you get your work done. You could just hire a teenage neighbor to come over and play with your kids while you work in the home. It could be a great babysitter training opportunity for a preteen if you stay in the house.

After-school care

If you have kids in school, you need to find care from the time school ends until you return home. Fortunately, many schools now have after school care programs. These programs, often called "latchkey," provide children with activities and homework assistance at the school or another location. If you do not have this option, you will need to find alternate arrangements. Check with your school first for recommendations. You can also check with local daycare centers to find out if they have programs for older children. You may also find a stay-at-home parent of one of your child's friends who would be willing to watch your children.

Summer programs

Many parents with school-aged children hire a babysitter to care for the children over the summer. Many college students see such an opportunity as a great way to make money over the summer. However, you may not be able to find someone for the whole summer. Further, you may want your children to get involved with more constructive activities over the summer. Many organizations offer summer camp programs to entertain and educate kids during the summer months. Some of these may be overnight camps, while others may be day camps. Many camp organizers embrace a theme and you can easily find something of interest to your child. Camps may focus on specific sports, arts, adventures, religion, or many other special interests.

Backup care

Once you have good child care in place, then work on backup arrangements. You may need them when you have a sick child, or when your childcare provider is not available. For example, if you use a daycare center, they often follow a similar schedule to the school system, so they may closed on certain holidays, or during inclement weather.

Relatives, grandparents, or single friends with flexible jobs make good backup care for sick kids. Some organizations also exist to provide sick childcare. They have nurses on staff and separate accommodations for the ill children. Parents with only mildly ill children find such an option useful.

If your childcare provider is not available, you have more options. You need to identify some alternatives, such as other babysitters or perhaps friends that stay-at-home. You may want to join your local PTA or some other parent group to make friends with other parents. You may also want to inquire with your employer or potential employer about kids at work. This doesn't happen often, but some workplaces allow you to bring your children along sometimes, particularly when your kids will just sit and read, do quiet activities, or watch a video.

Your Financial Needs

If you pursue a work option that results in reducing your work hours, you must consider how that decision affects your financial situation. You will lose income if you work fewer hours, which you can easily estimate. However, if decide to pursue working on your own or starting a business, you face more complex financial implications that you must consider. In addition to loss of salary and potential expenses of a new business venture, an alternate work arrangement could lead to a loss of benefits, such as healthcare insurance or retirement savings contributions. You must factor these items into your budget as well.

You should also spend some time thinking creatively about how an altered work schedule could change your living expenses. If you work less or you tele-work, you have opportunities to save money on childcare, clothing, gas, and travel expenses. You may also be able to dedicate more time to other things in your life so that you can also save more money. For example, you may be able to reduce your food costs by eating out less if you have time to properly plan meals, cut coupons, and grocery shop. You can also save money through doing things on your own, such as cutting your child's hair and growing your own vegetables. You may also want to make some deliberate choices in order to cut your expenses. Consider things you can sacrifice such as cable television, daily newspapers, expensive haircuts, or your daily latte.

Your lifestyle may allow cost savings in other areas of your spending practices. Take time now to sit down and draw up a budget. Include your projected income and your projected expenses and see where you stand. A written budget allows you to more easily identify opportunities to save money, allowing you to pursue the work arrangement that you want.

Chapter Wrap-Up

Regardless of the work situation you pursue, you can't do it alone. You need other people and resources in place to allow you to work and have a family. The more resources you have, the easier and more enjoyable life you will have. If you feel alone and do not have help, you need to reach out and find it. Many other parents need help, too, and by partnering with them, you can find other resources. For a family-friendly work arrangement to be successful, you must work to put these resources in place.

Resources

Child Care Resources

Babysitters.com: *www.babysitters.com*

A directory of babysitters with qualifications listed; you can search by geographic area, qualifications, and/or availability.

Child Care Aware: *www.childcareaware.org*

A nonprofit initiative committed to helping parents find the best information on locating quality childcare and childcare resources in their community.

Kid's Camps: *www.kidscamps.com*

A comprehensive online directory of both day camps and over-night camps nationally.

Nanny.com: *www.nanny.com*

Provides advice and resources on finding, selecting, and working with a nanny.

National Association for Family Child Care: *www.nafcc.org*

A professional association for home childcare providers. Includes a database of members that parents can search to find a qualified provider in their area.

National Summer Camp Association: *www.summercamp.org*

A free national directory of overnight camps for kids.

SitterCity.com: *www.sittercity.com*

A national database of babysitters and nannies.

The Sitter Café: *www.sittercafe.com*

Another database service that allows you to search for babysitters and nannies in your area.

U.S. State Department: *http://exchanges.state.gov/education/jexchanges/private/aupair.htm*

Provides information, resources, and direction on hiring au pairs.

General Resources

Work and Family Connection: *www.WFCResources.com*

The WFC Resources Website is a rich source of news, information, and solutions that will guide those who are working toward a more flexible, supportive, and effective workplace.

E-mealz: *www.e-mealz.com*

A meal planning solution that provides simple, family-friendly and budget conscious recipes, and an aisle-by-aisle grocery list. You can easily plan a week of meals for your family and quickly create a hassle-free grocery list to make sure you have everything you need.

National Association of Professional Organizers: *www.napo.net* Includes a searchable directory of professional organizers you can employ to assist you around your home.

Safe Shopping: *www.safeshopping.org*

An informational site by the American Bar Association that provides guidance in safe online shopping.

Thrifty Fun: *www.thriftyfun.com*

A Website with ideas on cutting expenses and creatively saving money.

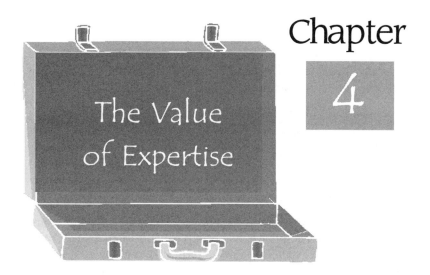

Chapter

4

The Value
of Expertise

As you explore family-friendly work options, you may find that more opportunities exist in professional jobs. That is, positions requiring a higher level of expertise tend to lend themselves better to flexible work. Even within the world of "blue collar" work, the more flexible work options go to more experienced workers or those with stronger skills. This does not mean you must be climbing the career ladder to the top of your company to get an alternate work schedule. It does, however, mean that the more expertise you have, the more likely you will get the work arrangement you desire.

How Expertise Leads to Family-Friendly

A high level expertise can lead to a more flexible work arrangement for a few reasons. First, many companies accommodate a flexible work schedule in order to retain a valuable employee. If you have a desirable skill set, or would be difficult to replace, a company may find it less costly to offer you flexibility instead of spending money to recruit and train a replacement.

Second, highly skilled workers who have demonstrated their abilities pose less of a risk to the company. If the company has confidence that you will succeed in a flexible arrangement because of your past accomplishments, the company will more likely approve your request. Holding such expertise allows you to better position yourself for negotiating a flexible arrangement.

The value of expertise pretty much holds true for any company and any level employee. For example, while in graduate school, I spent many years waiting tables. I think I was pretty good; at least I did well in tips. I have a natural ability to multi-task and communicate effectively with many different types of people. After I had a few years of experience, coupled with my natural service abilities, I could get more flexibility in my work. The managers assigned me to more desirable serving stations because they knew I could handle the pressure and keep the customers returning. My high level of expertise led to more desirable work, even as a waitress.

Is it worth your time (and money) to develop your expertise?

In most cases, pursuing additional expertise can be worthwhile. My current work situation exists because I have a high level of expertise in my field. While you do not need a Ph.D. to find flexible work, you will generally find that the better your education and experience, the more likely you will find a work situation that meets your needs.

If you don't have a high level of expertise, don't give up your plans for a flexible work option. Part of your strategy in finding family-friendly work might involve developing your expertise. If you haven't started your family yet, now is the time to get started on building your expertise. You can more easily pursue additional work responsibilities, training, or formal education before you have a family. I completed most of my work toward a Ph.D. before I had children. I found it easier to go to oddly-scheduled class times and to complete my research without little ones wrapped around my ankles as I usually have now. But if you already have your kids in tow, don't feel hopeless. Several developmental approaches compatible with family life do exist. I completed a lot of my graduate degree work after I had children. In fact, many times I creatively included my kids in my studies. For example, I had to do a lot of reading for my dissertation while my son was an infant. To accomplish this while still spending time with him, I read lots of academic papers to him. He didn't mind as long as I used my best sing-songy voice.

Do your research

Don't rush to sign up for graduate school just yet. You do not want to spend too much time pursuing specific expertise unless you know that it will lead to the opportunity you want. For example, many trade schools do a good job in marketing programs by highlighting careers that await their graduates, when in reality few opportunities exist. I spoke to a woman recently who spent a year going back to school to get a certificate in medical file management. However, once she graduated, she couldn't find a job in her newly found field in her geographic area.

Once you identify the career path you want to pursue, creatively consider your options on how to obtain the expertise you need. Or if you are already on the right path, carefully consider what kind of further expertise you will need. A few ways to identify the expertise you need:

✐ Arrange informational interviews with individuals in your target job (see more on informational interviews in Chapter 12).

- ✏ Talk with your current boss to find out his or her perspective. Or better yet, talk with someone further up in the company to get a high-level view of what you need.

- ✏ Do research with a professional organization in your field. For example, I belong to the Society for Human Resource Management. On their Website, I can easily find information about what skills I need to get different type of jobs in the field.

- ✏ Talk to professors at a local college. You might think that they will try to talk you into going to school, but you will more likely find them willing to share their expertise.

- ✏ Check the help-wanted advertisements in your local paper for jobs you have interest in. Pay particular attention to the type of education and experience they request.

Whatever course of research you pursue, make sure you identify what kind of specific skill development you need. Once identified, you can begin to work on further developing your expertise.

Opportunities to Develop Expertise

Once you know what you need, you must figure out how to get it. Many think only a traditional college education will provide the necessary expertise; however, many ways exist, especially if you plan to pursue a college degree.

Training programs

Depending on your pursuit, you may be able to find what you need within your current company; check out the training opportunities your company offers. Many companies provide resources that allow employees to earn certifications or take specialized courses. If your company does not provide in-house training programs, you may be able to access outside training programs through the com-

Developing Expertise

✎ Training programs.
✎ On-the-job experience.
✎ Certification of licensure.
✎ College courses or degrees.
✎ Reading or independent research.

pany, or on your own. For example, Karen found it much easier to get promoted once her company sponsored her for Six Sigma quality training.

On-the-job experience

When you have an opportunity to work on a new project, or help out someone at work, consider if it can help you expand your expertise. You can also seek out opportunities in new areas so you can develop further. For example, early in my career I volunteered on a team in my company that was setting up a new customer service center. It only took me away from my responsibilities a few hours each week and I gained much valued project management experience.

Sometimes you must make an extra effort to gain the valuable expertise you need. Linda, a divorced single parent, had an opportunity for a promotion at her job. The opportunity was a stretch for her skills, but she knew that with some extra on-the-job effort, she could increase her level of expertise enough to ensure success and have more flexibility in her work. So as summer approached, she worked with her ex-husband to reverse their custody arrangement for two months. She had the kids on weekends as her husband previously had, so she could work dedicated hours during the week. Just a few months of extra effort allowed her to successfully gain the expertise that she needed.

Certifications

Many fields have certifications that you can obtain to increase your marketability. For example, in the information technology field, you can become certified to work on different kinds of software and hardware. Having these certifications makes you more marketable. In my field, you can earn a certification as a professional in Human Resources. Requirements vary, but most often, certification requires you to pass a comprehensive examination.

College courses or degree

If you do not yet have children, now is the time to pursue more education. With intense study, you can get a degree these days in a fairly short period of time. If you already have children, however, pursuing further education can be a challenge. When already short on time, the idea of taking classes may seem impossible. However, many colleges and universities realize the limitations faced by adult learners, so they have created programs that allow even busy working parents to pursue a degree. Further, many companies provide tuition reimbursement to help support your pursuit.

Accelerated programs

Look for programs that target nontraditional students; many colleges have designed coursework that accommodates their needs. These often include evening or weekend courses and altered semesters that may be short and intense. Many colleges specifically offer accelerated degree completion programs that help adult students who completed some college coursework previously, but now need to wrap up a degree in a hurry.

Online courses and degrees

Online coursework can be a family-friendly educational option. Online courses allow you to complete your coursework on your own schedule. This might be in the middle of the night while your children sleep, on your lunch break, or on the weekends when you have your spouse or others around to help out with the kids.

However, do not pursue an online degree because you think it is the easy option. In fact, it may be more difficult. I have taught several online courses and students always tell me that they think online courses can be more difficult than traditional courses. Online courses require active learning on the part of the student. That is, instead of passively listening to a lecture each week, you must actively do research, write, and participate in discussions and other activities.

Not everyone will succeed with online education. You must possess a high level of motivation and desire to complete the program. Further, you must enjoy working independently. Most importantly, you must enjoy working on the computer, as you will spend endless hours doing so.

Carefully scrutinize alternate education programs

Use caution when pursuing an accelerated or online degree program. The Internet makes it very easy to establish degree programs that don't actually provide you with expertise. A degree from a bogus college will do little to help you find family-friendly work. First, it will not actually provide you advanced knowledge. The knowledge you gain from your coursework should help you improve your skills to increase your value to a company. Further, the degree is of no use if an employer questions the reputability of a degree you possess.

You can approach your search for a reputable program in several ways. Check out well-known colleges in your area to see if they offer an accelerated or online program, or at least a partially online program. You can also ask others' opinions. As you network and conduct informational interviews, ask people if they can recommend a reputable program. You may find that a company you have interest in has many employees who pursued degrees at a particular university.

Is it a "Diploma Mill"?

A "yes" response to any of the following may mean the program is not reputable.

- ✏ Can degrees be purchased?
- ✏ Is there a claim of accreditation when there is no evidence of this status?
- ✏ Is there a claim of accreditation from a questionable accrediting organization?
- ✏ Does the operation lack state or federal licensure or authority to operate?
- ✏ Is little if any attendance required of students?
- ✏ Are few assignments required for students to earn credits?

➥ Is a very short period of time required to earn a degree?

➥ Are degrees available based solely on experience or resume review?

➥ Are there few requirements for graduation?

➥ Does the operation charge very high fees compared to average fees charged by higher education institutions?

➥ Alternatively, is the fee so low that it does not appear to be related to the cost of providing legitimate education?

➥ Does the operation fail to provide any information about a campus or business location? Or is the address only on a post office box?

➥ Does the operation fail to provide a list of its faculty and their qualifications?

➥ Does the operation have a name similar to other well-known colleges and universities?

➥ Does the operation make claims in its publications for which there is no evidence?

(Source: Council for Higher Education accreditation, available at: *www.chea.org/pdf/fact_sheet_6_diploma_mills.pdf*)

Beware of programs that offer a quick degree, easy and cheap. To learn more about the quality of a program, ask to see a demonstration course or to sit in on a course that is currently in progress. Also, ask for an outline of the course content to understand the curriculum. Schools hesitant to show you what it is really all about may have something to hide.

Funding your education

Many parents do not pursue further formal education due to financial constraints. However, many opportunities exist to help support continued education. If you determine that the expertise provided by a college education will lead to the opportunity that you want, it can be a worthwhile investment. Even if you must borrow money, keep in mind that you may be able to repay your loans through higher paying work. Here are some possible sources of funding:

- ➯ **Tuition reimbursement.** Many companies provide tuition support as part of an overall benefits package (see Chapter 10).

- ➯ **University fellowship.** Many graduate programs offer fellowships to promising students. The fellowship typically provides a tuition waiver and a monetary stipend in return for service to the university. For example, I had a teaching fellowship to support my Ph.D. education. I taught undergraduate courses and in return, the university waived my tuition and I received a monthly paycheck.

- ➯ **Scholarships.** Many organizations offer scholarships based on a variety of factors. Several organizations provide support to parents, particularly women and minorities. College financial aid offices will often assist you in finding scholarships. Or you can use the resources at the end of the chapter to search on your own.

- ➯ **Federal student aid.** You can apply for federal aid such as grants (which do not have to be repaid) and low interest loans. The U.S. Department of Education Website at the end of the chapter provides complete details.

Reading and independent research

The movie *Working Girl* with Melanie Griffith told the story of a secretary who developed expertise on her own to move into a professional job. In the film, Griffith's character did not have the time or money to pursue a college education. Instead, she learned the business on her own by reading what professionals in her field read. In doing so, she learned her business and eventually came up with a unique business idea to propel her career forward. Of course the movies aren't real life, but we can learn from this example. We often forget the benefit of using written material to learn. Subscribe to a magazine or journal in your field. Go to the library and check out books about a topic of interest, or use the Internet to further explore your field of interest.

I thought writing a book would be a good way for me to do something meaningful while still making money and having flexibility. But I had never written a book before and had no idea how to do it. How did I get this book published? I created my own self-study project to learn about how to get a book published. I read books, magazines, and Internet articles about writing books. I networked to meet others who had published books to find out how to get it done. I bypassed many costly courses I came across that promised to get me published. Instead, I invested some time and a little money in a few books to learn the business on my own.

Chapter Wrap-Up

The more expertise you have, the more likely you will succeed in establishing a flexible work arrangement. It is worth your time and effort to develop your expertise. The more value you bring to a company, the more the company will work with you. Do your homework and figure out what expertise you need and what expertise is valued. Don't waste your time earning a master's degree if a company just wants a certification that you can earn through just taking an exam. And remember, informal learning opportunities such as on-the-job experiences and reading may be just as valuable as pursuing formal education.

Resources

CollegeBoard: www.*collegeboard.com*
A nonprofit organization whose mission is to connect students to college opportunities. Includes many resources such as a scholarship search database.

Council for Higher Education Accreditation: *www.chea.org*
A national advocate and institutional voice for self-regulation of academic quality through accreditation, CHEA is an association of 3,000 degree-granting colleges and universities, and recognizes 60 institutional and programmatic accrediting organizations. Their site provides useful resources on evaluating college degree granting programs.

FastWeb: *www.fastweb.com*
Free service that provides a searchable database of college scholarships.

Google Scholar: *http://scholar.google.com*
This search tool provides access to research and practitioner articles in a variety of fields. If you do not have access to a library, or do not have time to visit a library, this site is useful to conduct independent research in your field.

Occupational Information Network: *http://online.onetcenter.org*
The O*NET system provides comprehensive information on key attributes and characteristics of various workers and occupations. This is an excellent resource to explore the needed qualifications for a wide variety of occupations.

The Training Registry: *www.trainingregistry.com*
This site is a training directory that lists hundreds of training companies, trainers, coaches, training workshops, and training seminars.

U.S. Department of Education: *http://studentaid.ed.gov*
Provides a wide range of information for college students from selecting a program to finding funding.

U.S. News and World Report: *www.usnews.com/usnews/edu/elearning/elhome.htm* USNews.com's E-Learning Guide provides information gathered directly from more than 2,800 traditional colleges and virtual universities.

Chapter 5

Knowing Your Rights

Unfortunately, working parents have few rights in the workplace to help support the pursuit of balancing work and family. While supportive legislation is only a small part of what we need to create a family friendly workplace, we should not ignore our rights. Understanding your rights in the workplace will help you assert yourself and support your search.

Here, I will explain several important employment laws for working parents. I will first examine wage law, which has

Important Laws for Working Parents

- ☞ Fair Labor Standards Act.
- ☞ Family Medical Leave Act.
- ☞ Civil Rights Act, Title VII.
- ☞ Pregnancy Discrimination Act.
- ☞ Equal Pay Act.
- ☞ State Laws.

some implications for flexible work arrangements. Next, I will provide you with insight on the only current federal workplace law focusing on family needs: the Family Medical Leave Act. I will also review some nondiscrimination laws particularly important to working mothers and finally, will review the impact of state laws.

A government agency regulates each law and writes regulations for employers on complying with the law. The Equal Employment Opportunity Commission (EEOC) regulates discrimination laws, and the Department of Labor (DOL) regulates most other employment-related laws. Each agency provides more extensive information and guidance on its Website.

Fair Labor Standards Act

The Fair Labor Standards Act (FLSA) requires certain employees be paid minimum wage and also paid overtime (1 1/2 times their hourly pay rate) for any hours worked in excess of 40 in a given work week. The requirements of the FLSA cover workers categorized as Non-exempt. Workers categorized as Exempt from the FLSA are not subject to the requirements of the law. When you request an alternate work schedule that might affect your work hours, you must understand your status (Exempt or Non-exempt) under the FLSA.

Are you Exempt?

Workers qualify for exemption from the FLSA based on the type of work they do. Generally, many "white collar" workers qualify for Exempt status. The Department of Labor (DOL) provides specific details on its Website, but generally speaking, Exempt workers include managers or supervisors, professionals, sales people, or computer experts. Exempt workers must also be paid a minimum of $455 each week. Anyone paid less than $455 a week,

Exempt Categories Under the FLSA

✏ Administrative.

✏ Executive.

✏ Professional.

✏ Computer professionals.

✏ Outside sales.

(See *www.dol.gov* for complete descriptions of exemption categories.)

regardless of his or her responsibilities, is classified as Non-exempt.

Due to the overtime pay requirement, employers must cautiously categorize workers as Exempt or Non-exempt. Many employers try to avoid paying overtime pay by incorrectly categorizing workers as Exempt workers. Therefore, the Department of Labor has some specific requirements on how to treat Exempt workers in order to keep their Exempt status.

First, employers must pay Exempt workers on a salary basis, not based on the number of hours they work each week. This is an important distinction in the world of flexible work, because the employer pays the Exempt worker for doing the job, not for the hours of work they put in. This requirement creates some complexity on the employer's side to develop flexible work options.

Exempt workers also may not have their pay docked for being late or taking off early. Employers may only dock an Exempt employee's pay for a full day of work missed after they have exhausted all of their paid time off, or a partial day for leave covered under the Family Medical Leave Act. Therefore, an Exempt worker can have a flexible work schedule, because the employer should not track your hours worked each day anyway. Employers may have some policies in place on attendance, and can reasonably expect people to report to work on time, but the company cannot deduct from an Exempt worker's pay for a late arrival.

Reducing your hours

As I explain various work arrangements in Chapters 8 and 9, I will address some considerations under the FLSA. Moving to a reduced hour position holds the most consideration. An important part of proposing an alternate work arrangement includes identifying any necessary adjustments in pay, and your classification as Exempt or Non-exempt will impact how you are paid.

An Exempt employee reducing hours should simply have his or her salary pro-rated. For example, if you worked full-time (usually 40 hours per week) earning $1,000 per week, and you drop down to a 20-hour schedule, you would earn $500 per week. However, you receive this salary amount no matter how many hours you work. This often creates a challenge for part-time professionals who tend to work more than expected (such as at home or on the phone in transit) because they end up ultimately making less money per hour than they did as a full-time worker.

The organization can also classify you as Non-exempt and pay you by the hour, even if your work qualifies you for an exemption. Employers often hesitate to pursue this pay method, even though it works better for you. Employers fear you might take advantage of them by not working efficiently and working more hours than necessary to get your job done. Also, if you work overtime, they have to pay you the overtime rate of 1 1/2 times your pay. However, I believe categorizing part-time professionals as Non-exempt works better because you can make sure you get paid for all of the time you work. Further, it gives you more flexibility to vary your schedule on a weekly basis. For example, if you wanted to work a few hours extra one week and then take a week off unpaid, you would be able to do it.

Also remember that if your proposed schedule reduces your pay to less than $455 per week, then you become a Non-exempt worker regardless of your work responsibilities, and your employer must pay you by the hour. For example, if you receive full-time pay of $800 per week and drop down to 20 hours, your pro-rated pay should be $400. In this case, you would be re-classified as a Non-exempt worker.

Family Medical Leave Act (FMLA)

The only legislation protecting workplace rights of working families creates quite a challenge for employers. Due to cumbersome record keeping requirements and the unclear guidance provided on the Act, most employers cringe when they hear FMLA. Difficulties in complying with the Act have led many employees to believe their company wants to deny their rights. However, you must understand that most employers support the concept of FMLA, just not the challenge in administering its provisions.

The Act only covers companies with 50 or more employees in a 75-mile range, and eligible employees must have worked for the company for at least 12 months, and for at least 1,250 hours in the most recent 12 months. This works out to about 20 hours per week. You must consider this if you plan to move to part-time. If you do not work at least 1,250 hours each year, you lose your eligibility for FMLA leave. Many women drop to part-time after having a first child, only to later learn they have no FMLA rights for the birth of a second child.

The FMLA provides employees with up to 12 weeks of unpaid leave for the birth or adoption of a child. You also may take leave for your own serious health condition, or to care for a close family member (spouse, parent, or child under the age of 18) with a serious health condition. You may take up to 12 weeks of leave in any designated 12-month period. Each company determines the

12-month period, typically a calendar year or a rolling year (starting the day you use your first day of leave).

The FMLA allows you to continue your health insurance benefits with the same employer contribution while on leave, and also promises you the same or similar job when you return from the leave. However, you do not necessarily get paid for your time off. Many employers allow you to use vacation and/or sick pay benefits during your leave. In fact, some employers require you to use your paid leave benefits before you can take unpaid leave. However, you cannot use paid time off to extend your rights under the FMLA. For example, if you have two weeks of vacation, under the law you do not get 14 weeks of time off by adding your two weeks to the 12 required by law. Some employers may permit you to extend your leave, but the law does not require an employer to do so.

Serious health condition

The Department of Labor provides specific guidance on the conditions and circumstances that constitute a serious health condition under the FMLA. A licensed healthcare provider must provide documentation to allow your employer to determine if you or your family member has a serious health condition. A common cold does not qualify as a serious health condition, but a bout of the flu that keeps you out of work for several days and requires you to see a healthcare provider may qualify. Employee abuse of the FMLA has caused many employers to closely scrutinize requests for time off for serious health conditions. If an employer questions the condition, the employer may ask for a second opinion at the employer's own expense.

You may take your leave in one period, or intermittently. Therefore, if you or a family member has a condition that requires intermittent leave, you may be able to take such leave without penalty.

For example, if you have a child that has cancer and requires a weekly chemotherapy treatment, you could take just that time off each week to take her to the appointment, and then care for her afterward. By taking the time intermittently, you do not use up your 12 weeks as quickly, and you can continue working for a steady income.

Keep in mind you only get 12 weeks in any 12-month period. You do not get more leave for a different condition. So for example, if you use your 12 weeks for the birth of your child, but then your child becomes ill, you may not have any other leave benefits available.

Birth or adoption of a child

If you take leave for the birth or adoption of a child, you must take the leave in one block of time, unless your employer approves an alternate schedule. The employer does not have to approve the schedule, but some employers will allow you to take one block of time, and then take intermittent leave so that you can work part-time for a few months after you return to work. For example, you might take 10 weeks off following the birth of your child, then return to work and use the remaining two weeks by taking every Friday off for two months.

Both mother and father can apply for FMLA. While the leave for the birth of a child must be one block of time, it does not have to commence right at the birth of the child. So you could put off daycare for your newborn by Mom staying home and using 12 weeks of FMLA, followed by Dad taking his 12 weeks of FMLA. However, this does not apply if you both work for the same company, in which case you only get 12 weeks total for the birth of a child.

Laws Important to Working Mothers

Women looking for family-friendly work must also be aware of laws that prohibit discrimination. History tells us that women, particularly those with children, often face discrimination in the workplace. Employers may express concerns that female employees may not be as dedicated as their male counterparts, but treating women differently constitutes discrimination.

Civil Rights Act

The Civil Rights Act of 1964 protects the civil rights of the diverse U.S. population. Title VII of the Act covers employers with at least 15 employees and requires that employers not discriminate against current or potential employees based upon gender, race, color, religion, or ethnic origin. This means that you may not be denied opportunities in the workplace because you are a woman. The law also protects you from discrimination based on stereotypes an employer may hold about women. For example, if an employer refuses to hire you because you have children, and your employer believes that women with children lack the commitment of their male counterparts, then you may have a valid discrimination claim.

While I recommend talking about your family in the interviewing process, under the law, you have no obligation to discuss them. In fact, it is inappropriate for an employer to inquire into your personal status, such as whether or not you are married or have children. You do not have to answer questions about your children, your marriage, or your plans to handle your home and work responsibilities.

However, you must be prepared to answer an inappropriate question. For example, if the employer asks you how you plan to take care of your children while you work, what do you say? You may respond with a question, such as "I'm not sure how my childcare arrangements relate to my ability to do this job. Can you explain that to me?" Or if you would prefer to provide some assurance, you can respond with something such as, "I can assure you that I have everything I need in place to assure success in this job." If you'd prefer to use this inappropriate question to further explore the company's commitment to working parents, you could also follow up with "but, I would love to hear about the resources you offer to support working parents." If the interviewer brings up the topic, you might as well use it as an opportunity to gather more information.

During your search process, if you have reason to believe that an employer did not select you because you are a woman (or for any other protected class membership as mentioned previously), then you may want to contact the Equal Employment Opportunities Commission for guidance in dealing with your concern.

Pregnancy Discrimination Act

An amendment to the Civil Rights Act, the Pregnancy Discrimination Act states that an employer cannot refuse to hire a woman because of her pregnancy as long as she can perform the major functions of the job. Further, an employer also cannot refuse to hire a pregnant woman because of prejudices from coworkers, clients, or customers. The Pregnancy Discrimination Act also provides some protection for the time you take for the birth of a child. While not as specific as the FMLA, basically, the employer must treat a pregnancy-related leave the same as any other temporary disability. The employer should hold a job open the same length of time he or she would hold open a job for any other temporary disability. Finally, if a pregnant woman is ready and able to work, the employer may not refuse to allow her to work.

Equal Pay Act

The Equal Pay Act (EPA) amends the FLSA. The EPA prohibits employers from discriminating between men and women by paying one gender more than the other "for equal work on jobs the performance of which requires equal skill, effort, and responsibility, and which are performed under similar working conditions." If you believe you are offered less pay than men doing the same job at your company, you should consult the Equal Employment Opportunity Commission (EEOC).

State Laws

I have only covered federal laws here; your state may have laws that offer you additional protections. If your state law provides you more benefit or protection than federal laws, then the state law prevails. I suggest checking out your state government's Website to learn of any additional protections provided.

For example, several states have parental leave laws more generous than the FMLA. The National Partnership for Women and Families recently published a report on state parental leave laws. The full report is available at *www.nationalpartnership.org/portals/ p3/library/PaidLeave/ParentalLeaveReportMay05.pdf*

Chapter Wrap-Up

As a working parent pursuing a family friendly work arrangement, you must understand your rights in the workplace. Use this information wisely, and decide in advance how you will answer inappropriate questions. Defensiveness will only alienate you from the interviewer. A hostile response of "I know my rights" to an inappropriate question will possibly get you a very cautious second interview, but will guarantee the job to someone else. The hiring manager will perceive you as difficult to work with. If you truly feel you have been discriminated against, or your rights have been violated, you should contact the Equal Employment Opportunity Commission or the Department of Labor. The only way legislation helps protect us is if we exert our rights.

Resources

Government Agencies

Department of Labor: *www.dol.gov*
Federal government administrative agency that regulates employment-related laws such as the FMLA and the FLSA.

Equal Employment Opportunity Commission: *www.eeoc.gov*
Federal government administrative agency that regulates employment discrimination laws.

Books on Employment Rights

You Could Be Fired for Reading This Book: Protect Your Employment Rights by Glenn Solomon (Berrett-Koehler Publishers, Inc., 2004).

Every Employee's Guide to the Law by Lewin G. Iii Joel (Pantheon, 2001).

The American Bar Association Guide to Workplace Law: Everything You Need to Know About Your Rights as an Employee or Employer by the American Bar Association, (Random House, 1997).

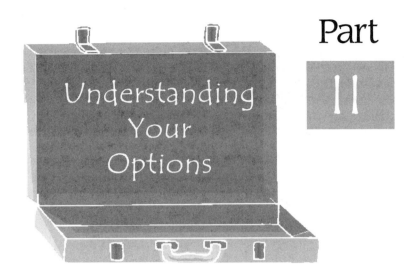

Part

11

Understanding
Your
Options

The Family-Friendly Workplace

As you begin your search, you must first understand the characteristics that comprise a family-friendly workplace. Several dimensions of a work environment create a welcoming atmosphere for working parents. For example, organizations often have specific policies and practices benefiting those trying to manage work and family. However, family-friendly attributes do not always appear in clearly written policies. To further confuse you, sometimes policies exist in writing only. That is, sometimes policies promise family-friendly circumstances that do not actually exist.

Common Dimensions of a Family-Friendly Workplace

Family-friendly work allows you to meet the needs of your family. Hours of work and some specific policies help create the family-friendly environment; however, some more subtle aspects of a family-friendly environment exist. In particular, a company's culture has a significant impact on one's ability to succeed in the company while working in an alternate work situation. The following sections further describe these dimensions.

Work hours

Whether a work situation will allow you to meet the needs of your family depends heavily on when you must work. I quickly determined that my flexible work hours make my own arrangement work for me. As mentioned earlier, for the most part, I schedule my work around my family's needs.

Your own schedule needs depend on your family situation. You may be able to work a regular 9-to-5 job, but need some flexibility to occasionally leave work early or come in late. You might want to greet your kids when they get off the bus in the afternoon. You may have no help, or very little help, and need work that you can do entirely at home. Whatever your situation, you need to figure out what hours you can work, and your needs for flexibility in your schedule.

Dimensions That Define Family-Friendly

☞ Work hours.
☞ Types of benefits offered.
☞ Organizational Policies and Programs.
☞ Other working parents.
☞ The boss.
☞ Company culture.

A family-friendly work environment has some kind of flexibility in hours of work, and Chapters 8 and 9 explain several different alternate arrangements. Work that requires rigid, never, or rarely flexible hours often makes meeting the needs of your family a challenge.

Benefits offered

Companies can offer several benefits to help you better manage your family responsibilities. For example, a new mother trying to return to work while continuing to breastfeed benefits from a lactation room. A single parent benefits from comprehensive healthcare coverage. Any benefits or resources that make your life easier help to create a more family-friendly work environment. Chapter 10 describes in detail specific benefits that contribute to a family-friendly environment.

However, you only receive support from these benefits if you meet the benefit's eligibility requirements. Often, employees working alternative schedules that are less than full-time do not receive benefits. Many companies only offer certain benefits, particularly health insurance, to full-time workers. A more family-friendly environment ensures all workers receive all company benefits.

Policies and programs

The mere existence of family-friendly policies typically provides family-friendly workplace evidence. The policies and programs also discussed in Chapter 10, such as a generous leave allowance and options for flexible work hour arrangements, suggest an employer's willingness to accommodate family needs.

However, keep in mind that the existence of such policies does not guarantee a family-friendly employer. Often, an organization will create programs in an effort to appear family-friendly, but only offer limited application of the programs. For example, Joan joined a large consulting firm that publicized its part-time opportunities for professionals. At the time of hire, her boss told her that once she demonstrated her value to the organization, she might be able to work out a part-time schedule. However, after a year of working hard and putting in extra hours, Joan came to the realization that part-time would never happen. The company claimed economic constraints and short staffs in response to her requests. She heard repeatedly that she could not work part-time "at this time." She finally realized that there would never be a time that part-time would work for the company and left.

The career success rate of those who actually take advantage of workplace flexibility programs also indicates the company's family-friendliness. Often, workers who request a flexible work option find themselves with limited future career opportunities. For example, her manager's offer of a compressed workweek at the bank excited Jackie. She could work 40 hours in 4 days each week. She chose Friday's off and made childcare arrangements for Monday through Thursday. However, after a few weeks in her new arrangement her boss started scheduling important meetings on Fridays and suggested that she should figure out a way to attend the meetings. She could not and as a result, missed many opportunities to get involved in important projects, and to meet with key executives. A later performance review noted a lack of commitment to the organization.

Therefore, you must be sure that company managers respect and use any policies that do exist. Further, you must find out the career implications of taking advantage of such programs and policies.

Anti-family policies

From a different perspective, some policies suggest that the company may not be family-friendly. For example, some companies put an emphasis on a restrictive attendance policy. The company might require a doctor's note any time you take a sick day. Or perhaps three late arrivals result in you losing your job.

Other policies make it challenging to manage your job and your family. For example, often you can resolve an issue at home with a few quick phone calls, instead of taking a vacation day to go home and deal with the problem. However, some companies prohibit personal phone calls. A company that does not understand the benefit of allowing employees to take care of personal business may not be family-friendly.

Other working parents

Success as a working parent in a company with few other parents often creates a challenge. While I respect and admire the first to forge a family-friendly work arrangement in a company, consider if you desire the role of a pioneer. The existence of a large percentage of working parents at all levels of the organization suggests that an organization is family-friendly. If those who will rely upon you at the company face the same constraints you do, you can more likely work together to overcome obstacles.

The boss

Do not underestimate the role your boss plays in ensuring a family-friendly environment. A company can have a lot of flexible work options and family-friendly benefits. However, a direct manager can limit your ability to use these benefits. On the one hand, your boss may tell you that you may not work part-time in his or her department. On the other hand, a supportive boss can work with you to create an alternative work arrangement even without a supportive company policy.

Further, you need to deal with your boss on a daily basis. Usually, you must talk to your boss if you need to take an unplanned day off or come in late due to a child-related emergency. The boss can make this an easy or a difficult process. Chapter 11 further examines "the boss" dilemma.

Company culture

The underlying values, beliefs, and principles that guide the behavior of employees comprise the company culture. A company's culture provides a sense of identity for employees and guides decision-making, setting the tone for the acceptance of parents who want to have more flexibility in their work.

I spoke to a friend recently about negotiating a part-time arrangement at her marketing firm. She laughed in response and explained that such an arrangement would never be welcome. Anyone who didn't work long hours did not succeed at the firm. The company culture emphasized the belief that committed employees regularly worked late.

A "best" company culture does not necessarily exist. However, certain types of cultures tend to welcome working parents. More often, casual work environments tend to welcome flexible work arrangements. Formal organizations tied to many rules and procedures often provide obstacles to creating alternate work arrangements.

A family-friendly culture often holds core values, such as a general sensitivity to the needs of employees, openness of communication at all levels in the company, and risk-taking tendencies. Companies sensitive to employees' needs will often be more receptive to ideas that help employees better balance their work and personal life. Environments that support open communication allow working parents to more easily voice their concerns about workload or other issues causing difficulty. Finally, risk-taking companies will more likely experiment with alternate work schedules.

Evaluating the Claims of a Family-Friendly Employer

If you plan to pursue an alternate work arrangement in your current company, you already know if you face a welcoming family-friendly environment. However, if you must conduct a search for an opportunity at a new company, you need to evaluate the commitment of a company to their family-friendly claims. Do not rely upon an organization's mention in *Working Mother Magazine* or some other media source to determine the family-friendliness of a company. Many companies claim family-friendliness when in reality, they do little to help working parents. Some companies attempt a family-friendly environment, but do not have a compatible company culture or trained managers sensitive to the needs of working parents. Fortunately, you can do several things to evaluate a company's claims.

Meet coworkers

Ask for an opportunity to meet your future coworkers. Look for visual indicators of family in their workspaces. Ask directly about the family-friendliness of the company. What does the organization do to recognize families? Are kids welcome at the holiday party? Is the organization flexible? Or are working parents penalized? Ask about a typical day. Is there a typical day? Is everyone at the office by 7 a.m., working through lunch, and leaving at 6 p.m.? The less you see a typical day, the more likely the organization welcomes a varying schedule.

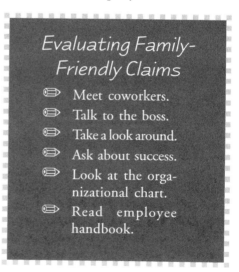

Evaluating Family-Friendly Claims

- Meet coworkers.
- Talk to the boss.
- Take a look around.
- Ask about success.
- Look at the organizational chart.
- Read employee handbook.

Many job applicants hesitate to ask such questions of coworkers in fear that doing so will leave a poor impression, jeopardizing the chance of getting the job. To avoid this concern, be subtle in your questioning. For example, ask if the company hosts social events, and ask about the last event. In describing the event, your future coworker will tell you if the event welcomed family members.

Instead of asking if everyone works late, try "tell me about a typical work day." Indirect questions can uncover much useful information.

What if you do slip and admit that you have a family that you actually love and want to see sometimes? Frankly, if this information causes a company to cross you off the candidate list, then you probably do not want to work there anyway.

Look for opportunities to get to know your boss

Consider yourself fortunate if you get the opportunity to lunch or spend some casual time with the potential boss. The more you can talk to a potential boss, the more likely you will uncover their true feelings about balancing work and personal life. Does the boss ask you about your family? Does he or she talk about family? Or is it all business talk? The willingness to discuss family indicates the boss likely recognizes the importance of family in your life. If he or she does not mention family, find an opportunity to mention your own children and carefully watch for the reaction. For example, if the day starts at 9 a.m., comment "my kids catch the bus at 8 a.m. so that start time works out great for me." If such a statement brings a cringe or surprised response, then you may want to probe further.

However, don't slam on the brakes if the new boss does not ask to see the latest picture of your cute kids. Concerns with employment discrimination charges (as discussed earlier in Chapter 5) cause many hiring managers to hold off on such questions. In such a case, rely on some of the other indicators to figure out the company beliefs.

Take a look around

A visual scan of the workplace can provide you with valuable information on the culture of the work environment. Are employees dressed formally or casually? Is the office quiet, or bustling? Do the employees appear happy or stressed? People happy at home and at work tend to show up in a more relaxed work environment. Look for indicators of working parents. This will include lots of pictures of children and proudly displayed young artwork. Look for bulletin boards and see what kind of information is posted for employees. Announcements of wellness or fitness programs provide some evidence that the company takes care of its employees.

You can also explore the company Website for indicators of family-friendliness. The look of the Website can help you get a feel for the organization. Many companies highlight the benefits they offer, or provide some insight on their company culture. You can also often check out the structure of the organizations. See if they have a department or a person responsible for work/life management. Many larger companies have someone dedicated to finding ways to improve the employee's balance.

Ask about success

Ask questions in the interview process about how the company measures performance. Do employees have goals to obtain, or does attendance determine success? Can your boss see how much work you have accomplished? For example, in the sales field, how much you sell determines success, and your manager receives sales reports so that he or she knows how much you have sold. The manager does not need to see the salesperson every day to measure productivity. The more a company values the actual contribution that an employee makes, the more likely you can succeed at the company by working hard.

Ask your potential boss or peers how they achieved their current success in the company. Are talents and abilities recognized? Or did they "put in the hours" and work a lot of overtime to demonstrate commitment to the company? Many companies expect you to pay your dues by working long hours in order to win a promotion. You will have difficulty getting by on an alternate work schedule in this type of company. However, you will get more support for your request if the company uses true measures of productivity to determine performance.

Look at the organizational chart

A flip through the organization's annual report or the organizational chart provides valuable insight on the organization's history of working with working parents. In particular, the number of women holding high-level positions in the company often indicates a family-friendly environment. As discussed earlier, women have traditionally taken on more domestic responsibilities, and, as a result, faced more difficulty in making career advances. Many companies boast comparable numbers of men and women on payroll. However, organizational barriers not friendly to women with children often prevent women from moving up within the company. As a result, companies that do not allow women the flexibility to meet family needs end up with few women leaders in the organization.

The employee handbook

Ask for a copy of the employee manual or handbook. Some companies might be surprised at this request, but just explain your interest in getting a feel for the company and your belief that the handbook will help you better understand how things work. Remember, the selection process should be mutual. That is, the company selects you, but you also must select the company as someplace you want to work. Therefore, you should not be afraid to ask for more information.

A read through the handbook provides valuable insight on company policies and benefits. Look for policies on scheduling work and taking time off. Examine the tone of these policies. Is it a positive tone, perhaps explaining to employees how to communicate their needs for time off? Or does the handbook take on a negative tone spelling out penalties for missing work? Look for the policies and benefits discussed later in this book. Are there opportunities for extended leave? Does the company provide a lactation room? Are maternity benefits discussed? If the manual describes family-friendly benefits, take the opportunity to ask how many employees actually use any of those benefits.

Chapter Wrap-Up

Gauging the receptiveness of a company to family-friendly work prepares you to request an alternate work arrangement. The following chapters will discuss the dimensions of a family-friendly work environment in more detail. Significant indicators of a family-friendly work environment include the dimensions of work hour options, policies, and benefits. However, you must also pay attention to the company culture and general atmosphere to determine if you can successfully negotiate family-friendly work.

Resources

Management Help.org: *www.managementhelp.org/org_thry/culture/culture.htm*
Learn more about organizational culture and different types of culture.

Fortune magazine: *http://money.cnn.com/magazines/fortune/bestcompanies*
Fortune magazine publishes its list of 100 Best Companies to Work For each year. They feature companies that rate high with

employees. In addition to their list, they rank employers by percentage of women employees, and provide a list of employers that encourage work-life balance.

Society for Human Resource Management: *www.shrm.org/ bestcompanies*

Provides a list of the employee-focused small- and medium-size companies.

Working Mother magazine: *www.workingmother.com*

Working Mother magazine provides an annual list of the 100 most family-friendly companies. Their criteria for selection to the list provides additional ideas in evaluating the friendliness of potential employers.

Catalyst: *www.catalyst.org*

A nonprofit research and advisory board that researches and recognizes businesses and organizations that provide support to women.

Chapter 7

Characteristics of a Family-Friendly Job

Ideally, a family-friendly company will help you create a family-friendly job, regardless of what kind of work you actually do. However, if your search involves a career change, you may want to consider pursuing a job that offers a high potential for a family-friendly arrangement. While many different jobs and career paths can offer flexibility, the very nature of certain jobs provide more opportunities for alternate work options.

How you feel about your job strongly influences your ability to create a family-friendly work arrangement. Work often takes you away from your family, and if you do not enjoy it, then you will only resent your work. If you have already found a job or career you feel passionate about, then do not leave it. But if you haven't found your calling, considering family-friendly job dimensions may help you identify a work path compatible with family.

When You Work

The more hours available in a week to work, the more likely you can find a work shift that meets your needs. For example, hospitals need staff seven days a week, 24 hours a day. While nursing and other hospital jobs often require working nights and weekends, you will have more schedule options, increasing the odds of creating a schedule that works. While many people do

Family-Friendly Job Dimensions

- ✏ When you work.
- ✏ Where you work.
- ✏ How you communicate.
- ✏ Demand for skills.
- ✏ Nature of the work.
- ✏ Other characteristics.

not have any desire to work the third shift, such a work schedule could be a good alternate for you when working out care for your children.

Jobs that allow you to set your own hours help you build a family-friendly opportunity. For example, many service-related careers allow you to make as much or as little money as you want by choosing how much you will work. If a hair stylist can find a salon willing to rent him space, he can set his own hours.

Jobs that allow you to work independently also give you the opportunity to work alternate hours. For example, like many consultants and college professors, I do much of my work at odd hours. I can grade papers, do research, read articles, work on projects, prepare classes, and many other activities at any time of the day. I often work a few hours at naptime and when the kids sleep at night. While I still have a hectic schedule, I can spend more time with my kids and only take them to the childcare provider a few days a week even though I work nearly full-time.

For parents with school-aged children, jobs that offer working hours during the school day can also be family-friendly. For example, schoolteachers' schedules often work out well because they work during their own children's school hours and enjoy time off in the summer with their children.

Overtime Work

The absence of overtime work helps create a family-friendly job. Exempt and Non-exempt workers have different overtime work considerations. Exempt workers may work hours in excess of their regularly scheduled hours, but they do not receive any additional pay for that time. Overtime work for Exempt employees generally occurs when they engage in special projects, or face an unexpected increase in the workload due to increased business. However, some Exempt workers regularly expect a lot of overtime work. For example, attorneys at many law firms regularly work 70 to 80 hours each week. Accountants typically face many extra hours during tax season.

Non-exempt workers receive an overtime rate of 1 1/2 times their regular pay rate for any overtime hours worked in excess of 40 hours in a given workweek. While Non-exempt workers at least get paid for overtime work, they often do not have control over when they have to work overtime.

Obviously, working more than the traditional 40-hour workweek can rob you of the precious time you want to spend with your family. Therefore, a family-friendly job does not require a great deal of overtime work, for both Exempt and Non-exempt workers. Further, when you must work overtime, a family-friendly opportunity will at least allow adequate notice. For example, if your daily workload depends on the number of customers that come to the business during the day, you may only receive very short notice that you must work overtime.

Where You Work

Obviously, if you can do work away from the company location, you can more easily arrange an alternate work schedule. For example, if you can do your work on a computer, or otherwise without being at the company location, you can work out a telework relationship as explained in Chapter 8.

Jeff works in sales and often has to travel to a client's site. However, when he is not with a client, he can work anywhere. So, when his son started preschool and only needed care two afternoons a week, Jeff altered his schedule so that he could work at home those two afternoons while his son napped.

If you must work onsite at the company, the location of the company in proximity to your home also helps support the family-friendliness of a job. If you have an hour commute each way to work, you lose two hours of valuable time each day. A 15-minute commute gives you another hour and a half to manage your family each day.

How You Communicate With Others

When and how you must communicate with others in your work can help create or hinder a family-friendly work arrangement. If you must be available to consult with others on a regular basis in person, then it may be difficult to have flexibility. For example, if you work closely on a team, you may need constant communication. Generally, if you have more independent work that does not require constant communication with someone else, you can more likely create a flexible work option.

Work that requires regular customer contact also often creates limited opportunities to flexible work arrangements. For example, a customer service representative who works with an assigned client base must be available to his or her clients often on a daily basis during regular business hours. However, if you can communicate with those you need to via the telephone or e-mail instead of in person, you may still be able to work out a flexible work arrangement.

Demand for Work

The more demand for your skills and abilities, the more likely you can negotiate a family-friendly work arrangement. If a company will have great difficulty finding someone to replace you if you leave, a company will more likely take extra steps to keep you from leaving. A demand for a particular skill often increases as the supply of people who hold that skill decreases. As less people decide to enter a particular profession, then the supply of trained individuals declines. For example, hospitals and other medical service providers across the country currently face a shortage in nurses. Because of this, many hospitals have sought creative ways to attract and retain nursing staff, such as providing more opportunities for flexible work.

General Nature of the Work

The nature of your work, or basically the way in which you get your work done often creates opportunities for a family-friendly job. The following general characteristics help create a family-friendly job.

✏ **You can work independently.** That is, others do not depend upon you on a daily basis in order for them to complete their work. The more work that you can do at your own pace, without having the involvement of others, the more likely you can work non-traditional hours or shortened weeks. For example, if you work as someone else's secretary, you will need to work when your boss works. However, if you do independent work such as a computer programmer, you may have more flexibility.

✏ **Your work is project-oriented.** Project-type work usually allows some discretion in the timing of the work.

✏ **You do specialized work.** In smaller companies where workers tend to have general responsibilities and no others do the similar work, a limited work schedule creates challenges. However, you can still create a flexible work arrangement in a small company if you do specialized work. For example, a small company may need a marketing professional, but only someone part-time because the small company does not require full-time marketing efforts.

Other Characteristics

Several other general characteristics make a job or career more amiable to a family-friendly work situation. You will find that some of these run contrary to others. For example, I suggest looking for high pay and low stress. These two don't always go together. Usually higher pay means more responsibility and more, rather than less stress. No ideal job exists that meets all of these characteristics. Rather, you should use these as ideas and sort out what you find most important to you personally. Again, you should not let these characteristics limit your options. Instead, consider them as part of your career exploration process.

✐ **Income potential:** The more money you can make each hour that you work, the fewer hours you must work to meet your financial needs. Typically, highly valued positions in an organization or in an industry pay more. With the higher level of pay, you can more likely afford to work part-time. Targeting higher paying professions goes hand-in-hand with having more expertise, but again, makes pursuing more expertise worthwhile.

✐ **Low stress:** High-stress jobs take a lot of energy. If work creates high stress levels, you need time at home to relax and rejuvenate. However, if you have children, you won't have much time to relax when you get home. In fact, you will often have more stress at home. Therefore, a family-friendly job will tend toward low or moderate stress levels. You will maintain your mental health, and as a result, be better able to care for your children and perform better at work.

✐ **Easy to measure performance:** If you can easily show how much work you do, you can more easily prove yourself in an alternate work arrangement. For example, if you process paperwork and you can report how much you process each day. Or in sales, you can report how much you sell.

Can Managers Make Alternate Work Arrangements?

Can you have a flexible work option if you manage others? If others report to you, your presence on a full-time regular schedule may be necessary to effectively manage your department. However, under some conditions a manager can work a flexible schedule.

Kim manages a department in the information technology division of a bank. She manages a staff of three full-time workers successfully in just 20 hours each week. She works two 8 1/2 hour days in the office, and at least one hour a day from home the other three days of the work week. Her arrangement works for her, but only because of several factors that fall into place. First, before transitioning to parttime, she delegated most of her nonmanagement duties to one of her direct reports. She also manages highly skilled technical workers that do not need daily direct supervision. She manages most of her employee's needs during her two days in the office, or with a quick telephone call or e-mail on her days at home.

Kim finds managing as a part-timer challenging and suggests that her abilities to delegate work and flexible management style allow her to succeed. Further, she has a staff that is capable of making decisions on their own, yet know when they need to give her a call. She ensures she is available when promised and responds quickly to concerns. Kim, similar to many others, demonstrates that managers can work a flexible schedule.

Chapter Wrap-Up

A job does not need to match every characteristic outlined here to allow you to create a family-friendly arrangement. These job dimensions represent many angles in which a job can more easily mesh with your family responsibilities. Many of these work dimensions encourage more interactivity between work and home life. However, many parents do not like the fuzzy borders, preferring a clear line between work and family. You must decide what works for you and pursue a job or career that fulfills your personal needs. However, you may find that integrating your two lives creates much more harmony in each.

Resources

The 2-Second Commute: Join the Exploding Ranks of Freelance Virtual Assistants by Christine Durst and Michael Haaren (Career Press, 2005).

Occupational Information Network: *www.onetcenter.org*
A government resource that allows you to research the skills, knowledge, and other abilities needed for hundreds of different occupations.

Salary.com: *www.salary.com*
A searchable compensation database that allows you to research the pay potential of a wide variety of jobs in different geographic areas.

Wetfeet: *www.wetfeet.com*
Offers insider guides on a wide variety of career options. Research based on interviews with those who actually work in the careers offers great insight on "what it is really like."

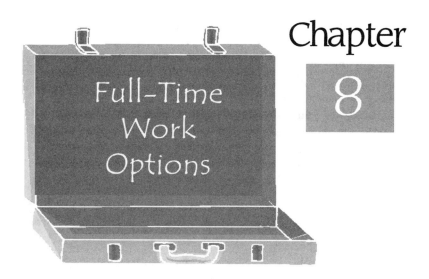

Chapter

8

Full-Time Work Options

Throughout the years, working parents and others pursuing more flexible work arrangements have partnered with companies to create a variety of working options.

To determine the arrangement that suits you best, you must first understand the different types of options that many companies offer. The following two chapters explain common options that exist at this time. However, only your imagination sets the limits of possible work arrangements.

As you review and consider these options, keep in mind that the nature of your work or the culture of a given company may or may not allow each option. Further, I have provided very general pros and cons of each option. For example, if you work in a position where clients depend on the ability to speak with you daily, a schedule that keeps you out of the office a day each week might not work for you.

Even if you find a family-friendly company, the company may not welcome all types of working arrangements. For example, a company may allow you to work flexible hours, but will not accommodate part-time work. Further, business needs may restrict a company's ability to provide flexibility. If you work at a bank, for example, you may need to work any day the financial markets are open.

Full-Time Work Options

✐   Compressed workweek.
✐   Flex-start schedule.
✐   Flexible schedule.
✐   Nontraditional work schedule.
✐   Tele-work or work from home.

The following section outlines several alternate full-time working arrangements. With a full-time schedule, you can maintain your salary level and benefits such as health insurance and retirement plans that accompany a full-time position. Also, a full-time schedule typically allows you to continue on your career track without delay.

Compressed Workweek

A compressed workweek provides an alternate schedule to the traditional five, eight-hour-day workweek. Someone working a compressed workweek works longer hours on fewer days. Several alternate schedules can be created with a compressed workweek. Some examples:

✐   Four, 10-hour days. For example, you work Monday through Thursday from 7 a.m. until 6 p.m. with a one-hour lunch break (and off on Friday).

✐   Three, 13 and 2/3 hour days. For example, you work Monday, Wednesday, and Friday from 5:40 a.m. until 8 p.m. with two 1/2 hour meal breaks each day.

✏ Alternate week schedules, such as working three, 10-hour days the first and third week of the month, and five, 10-hour days the second and fourth week of the month. This option only works for Exempt workers under the Fair Labor Standards Act (as explained in Chapter 5). Non-exempt workers must be paid overtime for working more than 40 hours in any week, which will likely discourage a company from approving the schedule.

Many parents enjoy a compressed workweek because it allows at least one full day off during the week, which provides some focused time with children and also some flexibility to handle errands not always easy to accomplish at the end of a long workday. Further, the schedule may help you find extra time in your week if you have a long commute. For example, if you spend two hours a day commuting, a three-day workweek gives you four more hours of free time each week.

On the downside, on your long working days you may have little or no time with your children. If you work a 10- or 12-hour day, plus commute, you may have to go a few days with little or no interaction with your children. Another complication occurs when you need to work on an off day. Often a meeting or other engagement must be scheduled on an off day and you must face the difficult decision of working extra or missing the meeting. Finally, a compressed workweek may cause you some additional stress as you may find yourself fatigued and not as productive at the end of working a long day.

You must take a few specific steps in order to make sure you select an effective compressed workweek schedule. First, choose your requested day(s) off carefully. Your manager will more likely approve your request if you consider business needs first. Is there a particular day that you face a heavier workload? Are meetings you need to attend on a particular work day? Your request will more likely be approved if you do not significantly disrupt work.

Next, you must establish your availability on your off day or days. Will you check e-mail? Can coworkers call you? Will you take files home with you? Having these types of things clarified, early on, helps avoid later conflicts.

Flex-Start Schedule

A flex-start schedule allows you to work a regular workweek, but start your day earlier or later than the regular start time. For example, if most employees work 8 a.m. to 5 p.m. each day, a flex-start worker might instead work 7 a.m. to 4 p.m. or 9 a.m. to 6 p.m. Many companies offer flex start as a benefit that all employees can opt into. When companies offer a flex-start option, they typically set "core hours" that all employees must work. For example, the company's policy might state that all employees must work eight hours per day and also must be present during the "core hours" of 9 a.m. to 3 p.m. each day. Core hours often coincide with customer needs and make it easier to organize meetings.

With a flex-start schedule you can find more time in your day by missing heavy traffic during traditional commute times. You can also have time in the morning or afternoon to handle things that typically happen during working hours, such as getting your kids on or off the bus. From a work perspective, a flex-start time allows you to work at times when others are not working. In my own experience, I've found that you can generally get a lot more accomplished in the early morning hours before your coworkers arrive, or after they have left in the evening.

However, sometimes not all employees take advantage of the flex start and may negatively categorize those that do. If you are the only one leaving at 3 p.m., and no one sees you working at 6 a.m., others may have the perception that you do not work as hard as they do.

To make a flex start schedule a benefit to you, try to establish hours that provide you with the maximum benefit. For example, an 8:30 a.m. start time might give you a little more time to get the kids off in the mornings, but you will likely face the same traffic as an 8 a.m. start. You may also want to consider taking a shorter lunch break to allow you to arrive later, or leave earlier in the day.

Flexible Schedule

A flexible schedule allows you to schedule your own hours. With a flexible schedule, you typically work a set schedule (which you set), and flex your hours as needed. For example, you might come in late one day after a doctor's appointment, and then work late the next day to make up the work.

A completely flexible schedule offers you many advantages. You can work as much or as little as necessary. You can much more easily meet your family needs if you have the flexibility to basically come and go as you choose. Further, you can vary your schedule, which may allow you to miss commuter traffic on certain days. You also can take care of personal business, such as your child's doctor appointments, without taking up sick or personal days, or eating into your valuable weekend time.

It may be difficult to keep your life straight if you have a constantly changing schedule. You have to stay organized and informed about happenings at your work. Coworkers may also perceive you as difficult to work with or, perhaps not committed to your job, if they do not see you there during regular times.

To make a flexible schedule work, you should set your schedule as much as possible, only varying when you need to, due to business or family needs. This will help you professionally because people know where and when they can find you. Further, you can plan your life more efficiently if you know your schedule won't change. For example, if you know you have Tuesday afternoons off, you can schedule meetings with teachers, doctor appointments, and other errands on Tuesday afternoons.

Nontraditional Work Schedule

Nontraditional work schedules include any schedule that does not fall into the traditional 8 a.m.-to-5p.m., Monday-through-Friday schedule. They generally exist in industries that involve direct customer contact. Retail, hospitality, medical, and other industries typically offer nontraditional schedules. You select a non-traditional work schedule by selecting a job that requires it.

You could have a set or varying non-traditional work schedule. With a set schedule, you work the same designated schedule each week. For example, you could work second shift, 3 p.m. to 11 p.m., Tuesday through Saturday. Or you could have a schedule that varies by the week or by the month. For example, in the retail industry, work schedules often vary based on customer traffic. Management posts each week's work schedule during the prior week.

A nontraditional schedule can be an attractive alternative for a working parent. For parents trying to avoid childcare, a non-traditional schedule can allow one parent to work while the other stays home. For example, if Dad works days in an office, Mom can work second shift in the hospital, leaving one parent to care for the children at all times. A nontraditional schedule will also often give you the opportunity to be home when you want. For example, you may choose to work third shift while your kids sleep. You can sleep during the day while they are at school, and then spend your other non-working hours with your kids after school.

Those who work in industries that have non-traditional work schedules do often serve the public, and as a result, can end up with some undesirable shifts such as weekends and holidays. Someone has to work in the emergency room on Thanksgiving Day. However, as discussed in Chapter 4, as you have more experience and more tenure with a company, you can demand the hours that you prefer to work.

A nontraditional work schedule creates the most family-friendly option if you have a set schedule. Even if you must work some undesirable shifts, if you know generally when you work, you can schedule your life around your work. Another benefit of nontraditional schedules is that you can often switch work shifts with others when you need a day off. If possible, try to help out others by exchanging shifts when asked. It's always a good idea to have co-workers owe you favors.

Tele-Work or Work From Home

Tele-work or telecommuting allows you to use technology to work away from your company location, most often at home. Your company typically provides you with the necessary equipment, such as a computer, desk, telephone, extra telephone line, fax machine, and office supplies. You work independently, dealing with customers or submitting your work via e-mail or on the telephone. You could tele-work full-time, or just one or two days per week.

When you tele-work, you completely eliminate your commute, which can save you hours each week. Even if you have a short 15-minute commute, you save almost three hours a week. Some people with long commutes find they save more than 10 hours per week. In addition, the flexibility to get away from work if needed creates an advantage over working at your company. You can run out and drop off that forgotten lunch box at school and easily work through lunch to make up the time.

You must have an excellent work ethic to successfully work from home. You must be able to focus and to ignore things that need done around your house. Some people do not enjoy working at home due to the isolation. The companionship of working with other adults provides one of the most significant benefits of working.

A challenge of working from home lies in ensuring you only work during your scheduled work hours. When you work at home, you can easily sneak away after dinner or while the kids sleep to return e-mails or finish a memo. A significant part of the work-life balance includes some time for you. You must make sincere efforts to only work your designated hours.

You can also easily be forgotten in the office. Even if you are a strong performer, if no one sees your hard work and commitment, you may be forgotten come promotion time. So, if you choose tele-work, you should schedule regular meetings with your boss or your coworkers in the office. You can easily get out of touch, and regular face-to-face contacts can ensure you stay in the loop.

Have a designated workspace. Don't try to set up your office in the middle of the kitchen where you have to put everything away at the end of each day. You preferably want a separate work-room with a door that you can shut at the end of the day and thus ensure that you have finished working for the day.

If you have an infant or preschool children, don't even think about trying to work from home without childcare arrangements. Trying to work without appropriate care creates a problem for both you and your kids. First, you can't pay attention to your kids and work at the same time. You can set them in front of the television, but is that really why you want to stay home with them? The quality of your work will likely suffer as well.

Chapter Wrap-Up

A variety of full-time work options exist that allow you to better meet the needs of your family. Continuing to work full-time allows you to continue on your same career path with your same pay and benefits. Doing so helps you create a family-friendly work arrangement without some of the sacrifices reduced-hour schedules involve. Further, you may find combining two options, such as a compressed workweek and tele-work, can help you create a unique work opportunity that meets both your career and your family needs.

Resources

Books

Breaking Out of 9 to 5: How to Redesign Your Job to Fit You by Maria Laqueur and Donna Dickinson (Peterson's, 1994).

Telecommuting Success: A Practical Guide for Staying in the Loop While Working Away from the Office by Michael J. Dziak, (Park Avenue Productions, 2001).

Websites

The American Telecommuting Association: *www.yourata.com/index.html*

Professional association to support those who tele-work or telecommute.

The Tele-work Coalition: *www.telcoa.org*

Promotes tele-work and telecommuting through educational opportunities, supporting technology, and advocacy.

Chapter 9

Reduced-Schedule Work Options

Reduced work hours may create the family-friendly work alternative you need. A shortage of time challenges most working families, and a reduced-work schedule could potentially lessen time-related stress. Obviously, however, a reduced-hour schedule results in reduced pay. Many parents cannot sacrifice the financial benefit of working full-time.

However, if you only want full-time work for financial reasons, you may want to spend some time evaluating your financial situation and calculating the cost savings of working part-time. As discussed in Chapter 3, often the additional time provided by working less allows you to save money on other expenses, particularly childcare.

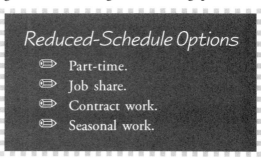

Reduced-Schedule Options

- ➯ Part-time.
- ➯ Job share.
- ➯ Contract work.
- ➯ Seasonal work.

If you do determine that reduced hours make sense for you, several options exist beyond simply part-time work. Further, you may be able to craft a creative option that involves combining more than one alternative. For example, you may work part-time, and tele-work one day a week. Again, you must consider your needs and pursue a work arrangement that both meets your needs and will also benefit your company. You can begin figuring this out by first understanding your options.

Part-time

A part-time work schedule includes any schedule option that requires less than the traditional 40-hour workweek. Some part-timers work only a few hours each week, while others may work more than 30. Many part-time schedule options exist. You can work two, three, or four days each week. Or you could work five reduced-hour days, or three reduced-hour days. Ideally, you should propose a schedule that allows you to meet your family needs, but also meets business needs. For example, Sandi recently took a position working part-time editing a magazine. She works one eight-hour day in the office and two four-hour days at home each week, three weeks out of the month. The fourth week when the magazine is in production, she works four eight-hour days in the office. This arrangement gives her the part-time hours she needs, but also allows her to fulfill her duties to make sure the magazine is published on time.

Your part-time schedule can be set so you work the same days and times each week, or it may vary from week to week. A set schedule can help you schedule your family needs because you know when you need to work. However, if you have an inflexible, set schedule, you may still face challenges if you have a family emergency or even an event to attend that you have no control over, such as a school activity that falls in the afternoon.

A variable schedule may give you some additional flexibility, but that may be limited if your company sets the schedule. If you consider a position with a company-set variable schedule, you must find out how much notice you will receive on your weekly schedule. Often, particularly in the retail and hospitality industries, weekly schedules get posted only a few days before the next week begins. When I waited tables in graduate school, the working parents always waited anxiously by the scheduling board hoping that management granted their weekly schedule requests. Ideally, you want a variable schedule that you set. You can control when you come and go, as long as you get your work done.

Part-time employees often face a challenge in determining the appropriate workload. If you transition a current full-time job into part-time, you must consider how to adjust your workload. Kevin told me that he started working part-time at his marketing job after the birth of his first child. I asked how the company adjusted his workload, and he told me that they didn't. He just figured out how to do his job in four days. He often felt overloaded and took work home with him.

I strongly recommend that you determine an appropriate workload in advance of making your request. Questions to ask include, *what could someone else do from your workload? Is there any work you do that does not really matter? For example, could some reports be streamlined or eliminated?*

If you do have a commute to work, try to work fewer, but longer days. For example, three eight-hour days instead of four six-hour days will result in an extra two hours of free time each week if you face a one-hour commute each way. You should also negotiate, in advance, how you will handle important meetings or other work that needs completed on a scheduled day off.

Job Share

A job share exists when two different people share one job at a company. They typically share one job description and one workstation. Numerous ways exist to split up the workload. Typically, those in a job share arrangement split up the week so the office has coverage of the job every day. However, many options exist such as:

- ✐ **Every other day:** One works Monday, Wednesday, and Friday; the other, Tuesday and Thursday.
- ✐ **Split the week with an overlap:** One works Monday, Tuesday, and Wednesday; the other, Wednesday, Thursday, and Friday.
- ✐ **Alternate weeks:** One works the first and third week of the month, the other works the second and fourth week.
- ✐ **Half-days:** One works in the morning, the other works in the afternoon.

A job share arrangement allows you to work essentially a part-time schedule while allowing you to possibly hold a higher level of responsibility than another part-time position might offer. A job share also helps you overcome some of the challenges of a part-time position. For example, if you work in a profession that requires your availability to your customers on a daily basis, your company will likely deny your request for a part-time schedule. However, if you partner with another person to essentially make up one full-time person, you can overcome this obstacle.

Along with the pay disadvantage discussed in the part-time section, a job share arrangement also requires you to rely upon someone else for success in your job. Often, your performance depends on your job share partner. You need to have compatible work styles and a positive relationship. Therefore, you must carefully select a job share partner. Ideally, you should try to find someone in your current company to propose a job share. If the company knows you both as reliable performers, the company will more likely approve your request. However, if no one appropriate exists, you may need to identify someone outside of your company. Or you may choose to partner with someone to conduct a search for a new position together.

Seek out other parents in your company to approach about a job share. You may want to consider partnering with someone with less experience than you in order to create a developmental opportunity for someone in your company. For example, if you manage a department, a job share with one of your employees may allow you to continue managing your department, and give a high-potential employee a chance to get some guided management experience. This could create a win for you, the employee, and your company. If you and your spouse work in the same field, you may want to also consider working out a job share with your spouse.

Your Job Share Partner Should:

- Share your work ethic.
- Have a similar work style.
- Have skills that complement yours.

It takes some effort to ensure that a job share works. You should take some time to establish ground rules to ensure success. Take some time to work out a written agreement to spell out all of the terms of your relationship. Some things your agreement should include:

- **How you will divide the workload.** Often, it will just divide by how the work comes in, based on your schedule. But if you do project-based work that has flexibility on how you determine when to work on things, then you need to establish who will do what, when.

- **A communication plan.** Determine how you will update each other on the status of work. You might leave each other written notes, voice mail, or e-mail messages. Or alternatively, you could schedule a regular telephone call or actually schedule an overlap in schedules each week.

✏ **How to handle decision-making relative to your job.**
Will you both consult on any significant decisions,
or will you just make the decisions that fall on your
days?

✏ **How to manage unexpected time-off needs.** Will you
just take the day off, or will you plan to come in and
cover for each other?

✏ **How to manage any needed scheduled changes.** For
example, if you face an increased workload and you
both need to work. Or if you need to exchange work-
days to cover for a needed absence, such as a kid's
school event.

Extra effort in determining your work arrangement before you
even request your job share will help you to formulate a proposal
that will more likely be accepted. If your boss sees you have thoroughly examined the work arrangement and have a plan on how to
make it work, it will make the decision much easier. Further, such
an agreement will make the arrangement more successful once you
get started.

Contract Work

This type of arrangement exists when an individual only works
for a company on an occasional basis. Generally, you may work as
an independent contractor from home, or only come into the office to complete designated projects. For example, someone that
works as a contract trainer may only come in to do a training
session once every few weeks. Working as an independent contractor allows you to schedule work when you want to, and at the
same time keep your skills sharp.

The work, however, will likely be unreliable. You will find it
challenging to convince a company to commit to providing you a
specific number of projects or work assignments each year, creating difficulties in maintaining your household budget. Also, you

cannot always guarantee that the timing of assignments will correspond with your family needs. For example, after Cathy decided to stay home with her new daughter, she worked out an arrangement for some occasional contract work. However, one of her first assignments came the week before Christmas, and the company wanted the work done as quickly as possible. Concerned that turning the assignment down might impact her chances for future assignments, she took it on, bringing a lot of extra stress around the holidays.

Many parents find work as an independent contractor with their current company. You may decide that you no longer want to work full-time and therefore, resign your position, but let your company know that you would like to work on independent contract projects as they become available. This arrangement offers your company an advantage over hiring a temporary worker unfamiliar with the company. You can also seek out contract work opportunities through doing research on the Internet, or through networking as outlined in Chapter 12.

Seasonal Work

Some parents find a family-friendly work arrangement by committing to a seasonal work arrangement. By pursuing work in a field that has a high need for employees during a certain season, you can gain income by working during only one period during the year. For example, an accountant could find a position helping out a firm only during tax season. Or you could work in a retail store during the busy holiday season. Although the summer may not be an opportune time to work due to your children, seasonal opportunities often exist during the summer months, such as working for a golf course, swimming pool, or other outdoor establishment. Depending on your geographic location, you may find opportunities in the hospitality industry if you live near a seasonal tourist designation.

Similar to contract work, seasonal work does not provide the same reliable income as a year-round position. You may have to make some effort to appropriately budget your pay. Also, while seasonal work may allow you freedom during most of the year, during the season your work may be extremely unfriendly to your family. That is, you may be expected to work long and inflexible hours during the season.

Determining Pay for Reduced-Hour Schedules

If you transition from full-time to part-time, generally your pay reduction should correspond to your schedule reduction. For example, if your company pays you $40,000 as a full-time employee, and you plan to drop down to four days a week instead of five, your pay should be reduced by 20 percent, or to $32,000. Some companies may insist on some kind of "part-time penalty." That is, the company may try to offer you a pay rate less than what you earned as a full-time employee. Such a penalty is not an acceptable practice. You must insist on receiving comparable pay, just reduced, based on your reduction in work.

You must also consider the impact on your benefits when determining your compensation as a part-time worker. As I will discuss in Chapter 10, some companies do not offer benefits to part-time workers. If you transition from full-time to part-time and forego benefits, make sure that your company takes this into consideration when calculating your part-time pay. For example, if your company pays you $40,000 plus full health insurance each year, the company spends more than $40,000 each year to compensate you. Let's say your insurance costs the company $6,000 each year. If dropping you down to part-time renders you ineligible to receive benefits, the company saves the benefit cost. You should consider that amount in your request. So, following the previous example where you reduce your work by 20 percent, I suggest asking for a salary of $36,800. That includes 80 percent of your original pay ($32,000), plus an additional $4,800 as a pro-rated replacement to the $6,000 in health insurance the company provided to you. To make this calculation, you must find out how much your company spends on healthcare insurance for you.

Exempt level workers (as explained in Chapter 5) must consider their exemption status in their proposal to move part-time. As explained, companies must pay Exempt workers on a weekly salary, even if they only work part-time. In the previous example, as an Exempt employee working four days making $32,000 each year, you should receive a weekly salary of $615.38 ($32,000/52 weeks) each week before taxes. But what happens when the workload increases and you work a few extra hours each day of the week? Or you start coming in on your off day, or answering your calls at home? As an Exempt employee, you keep receiving the same salary, no matter how many hours you work.

For this reason, I suggest that you request a forfeit of your Exempt worker status and ask for hourly pay. By doing so, you become a Non-exempt worker, but you can make sure you get paid for all of the hours you work. The company may hesitate at this request, because if you work more than 40 hours, then they would have to pay you overtime. But if you will truly be working part-time, you will probably rarely work more than 40 hours.

If you travel

If your job requires travel, determining your compensation becomes more complex. Often, when you travel for work, you work more extended hours during the days you travel. Victoria addressed her travel requirements in her reduced-hour schedule by looking at the month as a whole when determining appropriate compensation. She shifted from working five days to three days in the office during nontraveling weeks, working about 60 percent of her full-time schedule. However, she usually travels two times each month, requiring extra hours during those weeks. Therefore, she negotiated to receive 75 percent of her full-time pay for her reduced schedule. Over the course of the month, she estimates that she works about 25 percent less than she did as a full-time employee.

Pay for independent contractors

When negotiating your pay as an independent contractor, you must take into consideration your self-employment status. As such, you will have tax liabilities and you will forego other benefits. Generally, I recommend you mark up your rate roughly 35 to 50 percent. So, if you received full-time pay of $30 per hour, you should charge around $40 to $45 per hour as an independent contractor.

Chapter Wrap-Up

Reduced hour schedules provide working parents more precious time each week to spend with their families. As such, they create what could be considered the most family-friendly work arrangements. However, reducing your work hours also reduces your income, and often creates challenges in continued career progression. Therefore, you should carefully pursue this option and find work that allows you to meet your needs for both your family and your career.

Resources

Books

The Savvy Part-Time Professional: How to Land, Create, or Negotiate the Part-Time Job of Your Dreams by Lynn Berger (Capital Books, 2006).

Websites

Career Partners: *www.thecareerpartners.com*

A matching service for professionals seeking a career share partner.

Guru: *www.guru.com*

An online search site to find freelance and independent contractor work opportunities.

Internal Revenue Service: *www.irs.gov/businesses/small*

You are considered self-employed if you work as independent contractor. The IRS provides guidance to tax issues for the self-employed.

Womans-Work: *www.womans-work.com*

A complete flexible work resource offering articles, family-friendly employer listings, and a job share partner match.

The Job Share Connection: *www.jobshareconnection.com*

A free network to help you connect with a potential job share partner. The site also provides a job share proposal template.

Chapter

10

Family-Friendly Benefits

The presence of certain benefits within a company helps support a family-friendly environment. Benefits that help support your mission to work and raise a family can help reduce stress, making you a better employee as well as a better parent. An employer who recognizes the value created by offering such benefits will more likely provide the workplace flexibility you need as well.

Most companies offer some basic employee benefits, such as health insurance, in order to compete with other companies for employees. A fairly standard benefits package includes some paid time-off, basic healthcare insurance, and some kind of retirement savings benefit. However, many companies offer a more extensive benefit package to employees in order to create a competitive edge in recruiting talent. More importantly, many companies have realized the pay-off of offering a comprehensive benefit package. The more a company helps employees to meet their personal needs and manage their home life, the more productive employees become at work. Further, providing employee support helps build loyalty, leading to higher levels of employee retention.

Family-Friendly Benefit Categories

➯ Help with your children.
➯ Time off.
➯ Help managing your life.
➯ Career development.

Companies can offer a broad range of benefit options. Here, I will focus on benefits that working parents find particularly useful. An understanding of these options can help you evaluate the family-friendliness of a company by looking for specific offerings. Or, you may want to suggest new benefit options to your current employer. Understanding the options available will help you know what to suggest, and the ideas here will give you a good start.

The size of a company generally affects the type of benefits offered. However, even a small company can creatively find opportunities to support working parents. For example, financially it just doesn't make sense for a company with 30 employees to have an onsite daycare center. But the company could take a little time to research daycare centers in the area, and even coordinate a discount for you.

When asking about a company's benefit offerings, make sure you clearly understand your eligibility to utilize the benefits offered. Some companies only offer benefits to full-time employees. As a result, if you pursue a reduced-hour work option, you may not receive the benefits. Further, many companies have waiting periods before you can use benefits. For example, if a new job does not give you sick days until you have three months of service, you need to know that in advance. You can't ask your kids not to get sick, so you need to either ask the company for a possible exception to the policy, or make other backup care arrangements.

Helping With Your Children

Unfortunately, we live in a society not structured to support the needs of working parents in caring for children. School and work start and end times conflict, and limited quality childcare options exist. As a result of the shortage of public resources, many companies have stepped in to provide support for their employees. Companies benefit because if your children have the care they need, you can focus more wholly on your work. Companies can provide a broad range of support.

Childcare Facility

Perhaps the most attractive, yet least-offered benefit is an on-site or near-site childcare facility. Such facilities allow you to conveniently drop off your children on your way to work and pick them up as you leave. Some facilities also allow you to meet your children for lunch, or at least check on them regularly during the day. More sophisticated facilities will even offer surveillance equipment that allows you to check on your child at any time via a

How Companies Help You With Your Children

- ☞ Childcare facility.
- ☞ Childcare referral.
- ☞ Sick childcare.
- ☞ Flexible spending account.
- ☞ Programs for older children.
- ☞ Lactation room.
- ☞ Adoption assistance.

Website that streams video from the facility. A childcare facility on site can also allow breastfeeding mothers the opportunity to continue feedings instead of pumping during the day. However, childcare facilities typically only exist in larger companies that can justify the cost.

Childcare referral service

Companies without an on-site care facility can still provide assistance to working parents in finding childcare. The company can research local childcare options and provide listings to employees. The company can also educate employees on selecting care. In some cases, the company can partner with a nearby facility to offer employees a discount on care.

Sick childcare

A sick child creates one of the biggest challenges for working parents. Often, a child is just sick enough not to go to daycare or school. Parents become torn because the child doesn't necessarily need hands-on nursing, but has a contagious condition where they should not attend school or daycare. Regular or specialized daycare centers that provide sick childcare can help solve this dilemma. These centers place the sick child in a private room and provide care by a nurse or healthcare professional. Some services send a nurse or a nanny to the employee's home. Sick childcare can be less costly to companies than the alternative of high absenteeism.

Childcare flexible spending account

Under rules of the Internal Revenue Service, a company has the option of setting up an account for employees to spend on childcare expenses. This account allows employees to set aside pretax dollars from each payroll for dependant care expenses for dependents under the age of 13. The employee submits receipts for dependent care for reimbursement from the account. Employees save money by using pretax income to pay for childcare.

Programs for older children

Your childcare concerns do not end when your children start school. Schools close many days of the year, including the entire summer. Also, parents working the traditional 8-to-5 workday face a gap between the end of the school day and the end of the workday. Some larger companies may provide activities for kids, or at least an occasional opportunity to bring your children to work. On a smaller scale, some organizations just provide resources for working parents to find alternate care arrangements. The company can do research and provide employees with directories to after-school programs, as well as summer camps.

Lactation room

A company can often easily provide a lactation room for nursing mothers. A lactation room is a private room that allows a breastfeeding mom to pump during the day. Some companies provide simply a room with a lock. A more complete lactation room includes a sink with a mirror, and a refrigerator to store the milk.

For this room to be useful, the purpose must be dedicated to lactation. That is, permitting mothers to use a room dedicated to another purpose does not create a lactation room benefit. For example, Mary found that the security guard's office was the promised lactation room at her new employer. To use the office, she had to ask the guards (mostly male) to clear out and often found that she had to pump while trying to avoid their papers and leftover lunch on the desk.

Adoption assistance

Adoption can be costly and time-consuming. While the FMLA covers adoptions (as discussed in Chapter 4), employers have no other requirements to provide benefits to adoptive parents. In response to a growing number of families choosing adoption, many companies have added adoption assistance to their benefit offerings. This might include financial assistance to pay adoption fees, extra time-off, or access to adoption counselors.

Time Off

Parents need time off to spend time with their children, and also to handle unexpected emergencies. The opportunity to get paid for time off helps parents even more. Because Federal law does not require employers to provide time off beyond the FMLA, individual companies must determine what kind of time-off benefits to offer.

In addition to specific time-off allowances, some companies benefit working parents through providing some flexibility in using time off. For example, a company could have a policy that allows you to make up some time out of work instead of taking a day off. You can work late or come in early the next day to make up for a morning doctor's appointment.

Some companies also offer temporary tele-work arrangements to cover unexpected emergencies. Consider Chip, a quality assurance specialist with a software company. While he works mostly in his office, he can access his work through the Internet at home. Recently when his ill infant son needed to stay home from daycare for almost a week, Chip stayed home with him without using up his valuable sick days.

Time-Off Benefits

- Paid time off.
- Extended leave.
- Phase back programs.
- Extended leave.
- Vacation day purchase.
- Sabbaticals.

Chip worked while the baby slept, and also in the evenings when his wife returned home. Through this arrangement, Chip met the needs of both his family and his company.

Paid time off

Companies do not have to provide any paid vacation, sick, or holiday time under Federal law. Therefore, one of the first things an organization can do to support working parents is to offer some paid time off. A more generous paid time-off program will help you better manage your home responsibilities.

A general time-off bank that does not require a designation of vacation or sick time creates a family-friendly benefit option. This benefit is helpful because often companies have policies against using vacation days for last minute time-off needs such as a family emergency. Or some companies require a doctor's note in order to get your paid benefits for a sick day. A general time-off bank makes it easier to take time off when necessary.

Family-friendly employers also offer generous holiday schedules. A company can attempt to help working parents by at least giving paid holidays that coincide with school holidays. In addition to paid holidays, some companies recognize family needs, allowing additional paid time off to attend to family matters, such as volunteering at your child's school, or other community work.

Leave benefits beyond required by law

Some family-friendly companies offer extended leave benefits to care for children or for serious illnesses. Companies that must comply with the FMLA may offer options to take leave beyond the 12 weeks required by the FMLA. For example, some companies offer six-month or more maternity or paternity leave benefits. Parents benefit even more when at least part of the leave is paid.

Phase back programs

Many new moms as well as new dads take time off at the birth of a new child. But returning to full-time work after three or more months of stay at home parenthood can be overwhelming. This difficult transition leads many parents to decide to stay home full-time. To help with this transition, some companies offer the opportunity to phase back into the work routine. For example, a new mom could take three months of leave, then start back to work three days a week for a month or two before returning to full-time.

Extended leave programs

Some larger companies make an investment in parents who choose to leave the workforce for a few years to stay at home with children, in order to encourage them to return to the company when they return to work. For example, the consulting firm Deloitte & Touche offers the Personal Pursuits program that provides mentoring, training, access to networking opportunities, and other support to employees who take an extended leave of absence. This investment builds loyalty, so employees will return to Deloitte when they return to work.

Vacation day purchase plans

Some organizations give you an opportunity to take more time off by allowing you to purchase extra vacation days. For example, if you have two weeks of vacation, a vacation day purchase may let you buy up to five additional vacation days. You deduct the equivalent of one day's pay for each day you buy, and the deduction is spread out across your paychecks for the year. It works out so you take a slight reduction in pay in exchange for additional time off during the year.

Sabbaticals

An academic tradition for college professors, a sabbatical allows an extended leave of absence to rest, rejuvenate, or pursue research or other interests. Typically after seven years of service, professors have the option to take a paid year off to travel, research, and rest. Many nonacademic companies now also offer sabbatical opportunities to long-term employees.

Nonacademic sabbaticals are not often paid, but do give you an opportunity to take an extended leave every few years.

Help Managing Your Life

The stress of managing daily problems in life often keeps working parents from working efficiently and effectively. Enlightened companies understand the impact one's personal life has on productivity, and offers resources to support your need to stay sane with your hectic schedule.

Employee assistance program

An Employee Assistance Program (EAP) is a company-paid third-party service that provides help to employees on a variety of concerns. An EAP may provide counseling to employees on physical or mental-health issues, substance-abuse problems, relationship problems, parenting concerns, or even financial management. The specific services that an EAP can provide varies, but basically an employer subscribes to a service, and all employees receive a toll-free number to call when they need help. An EAP is a confidential service, and the company or individual managers never know which employees utilize the service. An EAP provides somewhere to turn when you need help for yourself or with your family. Whether dealing with a personal problem such as depression or anxiety, or just difficulty with a rebellious teenager, an EAP can help you manage outside influences on your ability to do your job.

Elder-care referral service

In addition to taking care of children, many parents in today's workforce also have responsibility for the care of their aging parents. Individuals often must assist elderly parents in finding someplace to live, or at least some provide daily care or support. Companies can also provide elder-care referral services. Similar to childcare referral, the company identifies local services and provides the employee guidance and resources to select appropriate support resources.

Concierge services

Similar to the concierge desk at a hotel, concierge services at a company help you with some simple errands while you work. This might include dry cleaning, photo development, car washing, or a host of other services. Some companies provide far more resources, such as onsite convenience stores or even cafeterias that allow you to purchase meals to take home to your family at the end of the workday.

Wellness programs

A wellness program may include a wide variety of wellness-related initiatives targeted at making you a happier, healthier employee. A company might provide workshops or resources on topics such as eating, caring for yourself or your children, exercising, managing stress, and other problems. Companies often provide this resource in hopes of keeping you healthy, which often leads to lower healthcare costs. But you also benefit through receiving guidance at work to help your personal life.

Many organizations provide programs specific to parents. This might involve setting up opportunities for parents to network, such as parent group meetings or an online discussion board. Or it might involve bringing in experts to speak to groups of parents about common problems in raising children.

Fitness centers

Many companies have onsite fitness centers or provide a membership to a local fitness center. You can often work out on your own schedule, perhaps having lunch later or coming in earlier, so that you can exercise before you leave at the end of the day. A busy parent with no time for his or her own health can benefit greatly from convenient access to fitness facilities. Improved health can also help you be more prepared to manage your family.

Career Development

Chapter 4 discussed the importance of developing expertise in creating a more family-friendly work arrangement. A company helps to support your needs

Career Development Support

- ➡ Training.
- ➡ Tuition reimbursement.
- ➡ Career planning support.
- ➡ Mentoring programs.

as a working parent by helping you develop your expertise. An organization can support your development in several ways, including providing opportunities to learn during your workday, providing you financial support, and providing guidance in your career planning.

Training opportunities

A company can provide a wide range of training opportunities. The more company-supported learning experiences you can access during work hours, the more expertise you can build to help you advance your career and increase your value to the company. Some examples of company-sponsored training opportunities:

- Onsite classroom training classes.
- On-the-job training from a more experienced colleague.
- Assignments to special projects or committees to build your skills.
- Online training courses.
- Opportunities to attend off-site training programs, such as those provided by local colleges.
- Financial support to attend conferences.

Tuition reimbursement

A company can also support your development through providing assistance in pursuing a college degree. Tuition reimbursement programs typically reimburse you for some or all of the costs to take job-related classes, or classes leading to a job-related degree. Often, companies limit the total amount of reimbursement each year. You must also typically earn certain grades to receive reimbursement. Regardless of the structure of the program, tuition reimbursement helps you develop your expertise.

In addition to financial support to pursue your education, a supportive company must also allow you to have time off to attend classes. This might include some flexibility to leave work early to attend classes, or access to company information to help with school projects.

Career-planning support

Often, a company can support your development by providing career counseling and guidance. A company can engage in a broad range of activities to help you plan and build your career. Some examples include:

- ✑ Access to career-planning books or other resources.
- ✑ Opportunity to meet with a human resource representative or career counselor to discuss your career plans.
- ✑ Assessments such as an interest inventory to help you determine your future career plans.
- ✑ Job posting program to allow you to apply to other jobs within the company.

At the very least, a company can coach managers in how to support the career plans of employees. A company can encourage managers to discuss career plans with employees, or even provide guides to lead them in their discussions.

Mentoring Program

A mentoring program pairs less experienced employees (protégés) with more senior employees (mentors) and encourages the pair to develop a relationship. Ideally, the mentor provides career guidance and support to the protégé. The mentor can share information about how to maneuver successfully through the organization. A working parent particularly benefits when paired with a mentor that is also a working parent. Such a resource often proves valuable in requesting an alternate work arrangement.

Chapter Wrap-Up

Beyond the organizational culture, the types of benefits an organization offers helps to indicate how friendly an organization is to your family needs. When looking for a family-friendly company, seek out information on the types of benefits a company offers. Identifying benefits such as those listed here will help you determine if the company will support your family needs. You will not likely find a company that provides all of these benefits, but you should at least seek those that are important to you. You also might find opportunities to provide input on the types of benefits your current company offers. This listing of family-friendly benefits should provide you with ideas on the type of benefits that you can request.

Resources

Employee Benefits Research Institute: *www.ebri.org*
Provides information and research about employee benefits.

Internal Revenue Service: *www.irs.gov/publications/p503/index.html*
Guidance on flexible spending accounts for dependent care.

Mentor Net: *www.mentornet.net*
A mentoring organization for women in science and engineering. Includes ideas and resources for starting a mentoring initiative at your company.

Chapter

11

The "Boss" Matters

A company can have a reinforcing culture and offer all of the right policies, programs, and benefits to support working parents, but without a supportive boss, you will never have a truly family-friendly work arrangement. To find family-friendly work, you must find a family-friendly boss.

Tricia recently told me she finally received approval for her request for a compressed workweek after asking regularly for more than two years. Tricia stuck it out with her employer because she loved her work and she didn't want to leave the company. But her long commute took too much time away from her young children. Four, 10-hour days allowed her to have one full day dedicated to her children, and also saved her two hours in commuting each week. What was the magic trick she used to get the change after two long years of requesting? She had a new boss.

Why the Boss Matters

Even if you join a company that supports flexible work, your boss typically has some discretion in determining if you can take advantage of such options. Tricia told me that her company generally supported flexible working arrangements. As a company recruiter, she actually hired many people into flexible work arrangements. But her boss didn't think a flexible schedule would work for her position. Most company policies that allow flexible working arrangements also allow managers some discretion in determining if such a schedule works for their own particular work group or department.

Further, when your family affects your work, you must deal with your boss. You have to call your boss to explain that your first-grader lost the homework he spent two hours working on last night and has now made you late in the frantic search to find the homework, and subsequently missed the bus. How your boss feels about your family priorities will make this an easy or a difficult phone call.

Further, your boss usually holds some discretion in determining how much flexibility you have on a daily basis. That is, if the daycare center calls to tell you that you must immediately pick up your ill toddler, your boss is the one who decides if you can just go, or if you have to take sick time for that absence. Or in a very unfriendly environment, your boss could decide that you will lose your job if you leave.

Your boss is also the prime (and sometimes only) contributor to your performance review. If your company conducts performance reviews or appraisals, they may be tied to promotions and salary increases. Your boss must be able to distinguish between real performance and just time on the job. One person may take a week to complete a report, while you can complete the same report in three days. Can your boss tell the difference? Does the boss actually measure productivity instead of time at work? If your boss believes your family inflicts conflict on your work, his or her opinion could affect future promotions and salary increases.

A supportive boss can make your life easier even if your company does not provide many family-friendly benefits. For example, a boss could allow a breastfeeding mother to use a conference room to pump in private if the company does not have a lactation room. At the very least, the manager can be supportive by allowing time away from work to pump.

A really family-friendly boss may point out opportunities for you to spend more time with your family even if you don't ask. For example, after putting in some extra hours on a special project, Andrea's boss told her to take the afternoon off because he heard that her daughter had an important softball game scheduled.

Why Your Boss May Work Against You

We've all heard stories about horrible bosses. The organization called Working American publishes stories of bad bosses each year. Among others, this year's list featured a story of a woman who almost lost her job because she refused to leave her son's bedside in the hospital to do a presentation. Many employees believe that managers get some kind of kick out of being difficult. The reality is, however, that most managers have accountability for the success of their departments. Often, the productivity and efficiency of a department directly impact the manager's salary and job security. This provides good reason for a manager to have concern for any employee behavior or requests that might jeopardize his or her hard work.

However, the biggest problem is that most managers don't know how to balance their need for productivity with your need to take care of your family. Most companies do little to train managers on how to manage with flexibility. Managers often do not know how to measure productivity beyond attendance, and do not understand the value of offering flexibility to their employees.

As a result, most managers think they must take a rigid approach in order to be fair to everyone. You must understand this motivation when asking your manager for flexibility. You will, more likely, succeed by empathizing with his or her need to keep you productive, and communicating your plans to make sure he or she succeeds.

Some women mistakenly target other working moms as a potential boss. It makes sense; work for someone facing the same challenges as you, and she will understand your needs. Right? Actually, you could be wrong on this one. Being a woman, or even a working mother, does not guarantee a family-friendly boss. Many women in management roles today have worked very hard to get to the level of manager, often without the opportunity for a flexible schedule. Some women in this position will work hard to create new opportunities for other mothers, but many won't. Some working mothers believe that, if they do not act the same way as men, they won't be taken seriously as a manager. Or some women just have the I-did-it-so-you-can-too attitude. Perhaps they weren't given any exceptions and they don't want you to have any, either. Also, remember that many people just have different ideas and priorities in raising their children. Just because you think you should attend all of your son's soccer games does not mean that every other parent feels the same way.

Men may find it even more challenging to find a boss that is supportive of family needs. Many people still hold on to stereotypes of men's and women's roles at home. A request from a man for an alternate work arrangement will catch many managers off guard. You may even find that your boss will not approve your request, even though some women in your department work flexible schedules. If you cannot convince your boss to allow you flexibility when women in your company have the opportunity for flexibility, you may need to move on to another company. However, if you want to fight for your rights, remember that gender discrimination law works both ways. The Civil Rights Act does not just protect women. That is, your company cannot deny you an opportunity because of your gender. A company cannot offer flexible work to women, and not to men.

Because many managers may be less than supportive, you must approach your need for family-friendly work with caution and preparation. If you need to make your request to your current boss, you likely know what to expect, but I will provide you with some tips to help you be more successful in your request. If your search will take you to a new opportunity, some ideas follow to help you evaluate a potential new boss.

Working With Your Current Boss

Before you can make a request for a family-friendly work arrangement, you must have your boss on your side. If you have worked for the same boss for a while, you probably know about his or her history in managing with flexibility. If you don't know whether or not your boss will accept a family-friendly request, your must first find out.

Past behavior typically predicts future behavior. If you do not know of anyone your boss currently manages that works a flexible schedule, try to find out if he or she has ever managed someone with a flexible schedule in the past. Ask others that have been with your company longer. Check in with your Human Resource department to see if they can provide you with some insight. But first, make sure you can trust your Human Resource representative not to share your interests with your manager until you make your request.

As you do your research and prepare your request, make sure you're performing at your best. Your boss will more likely grant your request if you have proven yourself as a top performer. Turn in assignments early, and exceed customer expectations whenever you can. The more your boss likes and respects you, the more likely he or she will support you.

Remember that your boss wants success in his or her job. There-fore, as you work with your boss, always keep their needs and interests in mind; your boss most likely wants to keep his or her boss happy. If your organization offers skip-level meetings, take advantage of this opportunity. A skip-level meeting occurs when the company encourages employees to meet with managers a level above their own manager. Upper management offers skip-level meetings to help you learn more about the company, and also to give higher-level managers a chance to get to know and collect feedback from more employees. By meeting with his or her man-ager, you can better understand what your boss does, so that you can help make his or her job easier.

Evaluating a Potential Boss

You may be in a position to evaluate a potential boss. In this case, you must make every effort to get to know this person. Be prepared to ask questions at the conclusion of the interview. If you have an opportunity to have lunch or dinner with him or her, jump on it. Getting to know your new boss in a more relaxed social setting will give you a lot of insight.

Ask your potential new boss about your future peers. How much does he or she know about them? Does he or she seem to know about them? Does he or she value real performance? Or does he or she just talk about them being reliable? A good working relationship with subordinates is a good sign.

If you receive a job offer after only one interview with your new boss, ask for another meeting before you accept the position. Many people think they have to decide on the job the minute they receive the phone call with an offer; this is not true. The company took time in deciding whether or not to offer you the position, so, therefore, you can take time to decide if you want to take the position. Explain that you intend to make a long-term commitment to the company, and want to make sure that you have all of your questions answered before you make such a commitment. Some questions you should ask are:

- **How is performance measured?** You want to know if he or she has some way of measuring your performance beyond attendance. If you get a response such as "well as long as I see everyone here working every day, I know everyone is doing fine," run!

- **Is overtime work common? If so, how much notice do you give when overtime work is needed?** If the job you seek may require overtime, you must find out your potential boss's opinion on overtime requests. Required overtime work with little or no advance notice can create many problems in balancing your family needs.

- **How do you communicate with your employees?** You want to know if he or she has some flexibility in the way they communicate. Do all communications take place face to face? Do you need to meet with your boss every day? Or do employees work independently?

- **What traits do you value in an employee?** Here the boss should talk about specific skills or abilities. If the response focuses on physical presence, such as "I value employees show up on time for work," then the manager may not value true performance.

- **How would you describe your management style?** If his or her response focuses too much on following the rules or ensuring compliance, then you might not be with someone capable of offering flexibility.

- **What kind of benefits does the company offer?** See if your potential new boss mentions any family-friendly benefits. If the company has them, and he or she is aware of them, that is a good sign.

- **Why did the person who held this job before leave?** This question can give you some more insight on your potential boss's relationships with subordinates.

Does he or she really know why the previous person left? Also, it is a good sign if the person left for a promotion within the same company. Companies that promote from within often have effective management practices.

Also, ask for an opportunity to meet with peers that work for the same manager. After all, you will work with these people on a daily basis. You most likely dated your spouse for at least a few months before getting married. You may spend more time with your coworkers than your spouse, so you should at least meet them before you make a decision. You can use this opportunity to find out if any of your potential peers has children. You will have more success following the lead of other working parents in your department. Ask your coworkers directly about your potential boss.

- ✐ **What is it like to work with the boss?** Find out if they like or dislike the boss. You will have to look for subtle indications, as current employees will not likely speak poorly about their current boss to someone they do not know.

- ✐ **Does everyone get along well in the department?** Try to find out if the boss plays favorites, or if he or she respects everyone.

- ✐ **Why did the previous employee leave?** See if the coworker's reason matches what the boss says.

Use the same caution in questioning the coworkers as the boss. You don't want to appear overly concerned with taking time off. Remember, the coworkers might have a very good relationship with the boss and will possibly share anything you tell them or ask them.

Chapter Wrap-Up

Many managers may want to offer flexibility, but lack the training and direction to help you manage a flexible work situation. A current or potential boss may be willing to help you work out a schedule, but ultimately, you need to take ownership and work out all of the details. However, your relationship with your boss will determine how successful your alternate work arrangement turns out.

Resources

Websites

Badbossology: *www.badbossology.com*
Badbossology.com features completely free access to more than 1,200 articles and resources on solving problems with difficult managers.

Books

Coping with Toxic Managers, Subordinates...And Other Difficult People by Roy H. Lubit (Prentice Hall, 2003).

How to Work for an Idiot: Survive and Thrive Without Killing Your Boss by John Hoover (Career Press, 2004).

A Survival Guide for Working With Bad Bosses: Dealing With Bullies, Idiots, back-stabbers, And Other Managers from Hell by Gini Graham, Ph.D. (AMACOM, 2005).

Conducting
Your
Search

Part

III

Chapter 12

Networking for Success

The old adage "it's not what you know, it's who you know" applies more to the job search than any other venture. Networking is the process of building mutually beneficial relationships. Your job search network includes the people you know that might be able to connect you to the right work opportunity. This valuable connection could be anyone, from your spouse to the cashier at the coffee house you stop at each morning. You can make your network work for you in the job search through actively engaging in building and using it.

Networking is key to creating a family-friendly work arrangement. Whether you search for a job with a new company, move to another job within your company, go out on your own, or even choose to stay at home for a while, your network will help you find success in your pursuit.

Building Your Network

Before you start expanding your network, you should first identify your current network. You can accomplish this by simply writing it down. Start closest to you and work out. First, list all of your family members. This includes your sister, as well as your Aunt Helen that you only see at the annual family reunion. Next, move on to your friends. Start with your friends that you see regularly and then work back to those who you have not seen in awhile. List all of your old friends, even those you no longer keep up with, such as high school pals or old college friends.

Write down your work colleagues, current and past. Note the people you know in your neighborhood and in the local PTA, or any other group you belong to. Next, consider people you know because you encounter them on some kind of regular basis. This includes your dentist, your eye doctor, your bank teller, and the coffee shop cashier I mentioned earlier. Very quickly you will have hundreds of people listed.

Who is in your network?

- Close family members.
- Distant family members.
- Friends you see regularly.
- Friends you see occasionally.
- Friends with whom you've lost touch.
- Your neighbors.
- Your old neighbors.
- Accountant.
- Doctors.
- Dentist.
- Current colleagues.
- Previous colleagues.
- Librarian.
- Hairdresser.
- Coffee shop cashier.
- Your child's friends' parents.
- PTA members.

After you have identified your current network, you can work to expand it. To do this, you need to put yourself in a position to meet new people. What kinds of people should you try to meet? Ultimately, you must target people working at companies where you want to work. Therefore, to identify potential network contacts, you need to reach out in a variety of ways, both professionally and socially. You should always be thinking about networking and your search. Always carry your resume with you, or at least some business cards with your contact information. You may find a good contact waiting in line in the grocery store, or while waiting to pick up your kids at preschool.

From a professional perspective, you can start with any professional association in your field of training or targeted career field. For example, I built much of my network through my affiliation with the Society for Human Resource Management. The local chapter holds luncheon meetings that I attend regularly. If such a group does not exist, or even if it does, consider other groups as well. For example, several women's networking groups exist, such as the Business and Professional Women's Association, or the National Association of Female Executives. You may also want to check out civic groups, such as a local chamber of commerce or a nonprofit organization related to your field. However, you can't just sign up for the mailing list and expect to get new contacts. You must become involved and actively network at meetings.

Tips for networking success at professional meetings

1. Sit with someone you do not know. You may be more comfortable sitting with someone you already know, but you should try to meet someone new.

2. Set a goal on how many new contacts you want to make. Three new contacts at a luncheon meeting is a reasonable goal.

3. If possible, get a membership list in advance, so you can try to target individuals from specific companies of interest.

4. Arrive early, and plan to stay late. You will make the most new contacts before and after a meeting.

5. Volunteer within the organization. You can make strong contacts by working with someone on a committee or project. For example, you can make many new contacts by volunteering to work the registration table at an event.

You can also find many new contacts at social gatherings. Often, a more casual setting with some cocktails creates an environment for more open conversations. The next time you receive an invitation to a party, consider who else might be invited that might be worth your time to meet. Once you arrive, make an effort to talk to people you haven't met before. Identify a location at the event, such as the food table or the bar, where you will likely meet people due to traffic. Be prepared to start the conversation by asking a simple question, "Have you tried the cheese dip? It's wonderful." Sounds cheesy, right? Well, at least it gets the conversation started. I try to read the daily newspaper before a social event as well. "Did you see the story today about the woman who rescued her dog?" also makes a good conversation starter.

Networking in your current company

You can use your network even when requesting an alternate work arrangement in your current company. Internal network contacts can help you gather ideas on how to approach a family-friendly work request. Others within your company can also help you identify managers in other departments willing to work with a flexible schedule.

To build your network within your company, make an effort to meet others outside of your department. If your company has a lunchroom, try sitting with someone new. Volunteer to help out with the committee planning the next company party. If your company hosts lunches or networking events for working parents, make sure you attend. If no such events exist, consider starting a parents group. A network of working parents within your company can help convince the company to offer more family-friendly benefits or programs.

Talking about your family

Many parents hesitate to mention that they have a family when networking with others, particularly in a professional setting. Many parents, and women in particular, have been stereotyped as uncommitted to their work if they focus too much on family. As long as you don't overdo it, talking about family issues can help you identify network contacts willing to support your family-friendly pursuits. Talking too much about kids will lead someone to question your work interests. However, a comment such as, "Last week was crazy, I completed a 20-page research report, traveled to two new client sites, and organized a birthday party to entertain six restless three-year-olds!" will surely evoke empathy from others. Once again, these subtle hints that you like your family and want to spend time with them may eliminate you from the competition for certain jobs at certain companies. However, you most likely don't want to work for a company that avoids you because you admit you have children.

Keeping Your Network Active

You must tap in to your network to make it useful. As you work on building your network during your job search, you will naturally share details of your search for a new position by informing new contacts about the kind of opportunity you seek. You must also work the network you already have in place. Chapter 13 will guide you in using your network in your job search.

However, you should work on keeping your network active even before your job search starts. The best referrals come from people who feel they know you well, or at least have known you for some time. Over time, you will develop relationships with those in your network through actively keeping in touch. However, you can jump start a relationship through conducting an informational interview.

The informational interview

An informational interview can quickly cultivate a new contact. Through this brief, professional meeting you hold with a new contact, you learn more about the contact or the company where he or she works. If you meet a valuable contact for you, ask him or her if they can avail themselves for an informational interview. You will find out that people generally enjoy talking about themselves, and you will rarely be turned down.

Treat an informational interview just as you would a real interview, but you ask the questions. Ask about the individual's job responsibility and his or her career path. Ask questions about the company; this information will prove useful to you as you continue your search. You may learn about current or future opportunities at the company, and possibly determine the family- friendliness of the company.

Be cautious though; even though this is not a true job interview, the impression you make during an informational interview can affect your future prospects at a company. Make sure you dress and act in a professional manner. Don't ask for a job, or ask the person to forward on your resume. Instead, keep the exchange informational and as brief as possible, respecting the interviewee's

Sample Informal Interview Questions

➨ Tell me about your job here.

➨ What is a typical day like for you?

➨ Tell me about your career path to get to this position.

➨ What are your future opportunities at this company?

➨ What do you like about this company?

➨ What skills or abilities are important in your position?

➨ What are important factors that contribute to success at the company?

➨ How does your company recruit new hires?

➨ What advice do you have for someone just starting off in this field?

➨ Does your company provide any resources for working parents?

time. Send a thank-you note quickly after the interview. If the interviewee did not ask for your resume when you met, you can send it along with your thank-you note.

Other strategies to keep in touch with your network

Try to arrange an occasional lunch or coffee meeting with important contacts. Use the time as an opportunity to talk more about the opportunity you want. You can also use a meeting to ask your contact for referrals to other contacts that might be helpful to you. If you see a contact at a professional meeting or a conference, make an effort to at least say hello. An occasional e-mail message also helps keep a network up to date.

Sample E-mail Message: Keeping in Touch

To: Beth S.

From: Jane F.

Subject: Touching Base

Dear Beth,

Just a quick note to say hello. The last time we spoke you were working on the big grant application. I hope that turned out well for you. Keeping busy here, I am continuing to do contract work through a local consulting firm, and I plan to start looking for a full-time position later this year. I can't believe summer is almost here! Drop me a note when you have time to catch up.

Jane

Keep your written network list up to date. I suggest keeping a networking notebook or spreadsheet file where you list all of your contacts. For newer, or less-familiar contacts, make sure to note how you met them and the last time you spoke with them. Notes can help with follow-up e-mails similar to the sample provided. Make notes about the current work projects, volunteer activities, or anything the contact told you about kids. A nice sign-off to a keeping in touch note might be "I hope Susie is enjoying her first year of school!"

Remember that networking should be a mutually beneficial process. Seek out opportunities to help others. If you hear of a position that might be a great opportunity for someone, go through your network list to see if you can find anyone that might have interest. People remember you more when they know that you have tried to help them out.

In your networking activities, you may find others looking for new opportunities. Consider creating a partnership with them to share resources. I suggest meeting other job seekers regularly for coffee, lunch, or a play date to share leads or networking ideas. Such group meetings can also help motivate you to keep moving forward in your search.

Finally, you must thank the people who have helped you. These days, people rarely take the time to handwrite a personal thank-you note, and your efforts will mark your contact's memory. Thank people for anything they do to help you, including sharing a contact name with you or introducing you to your new boss. You never know when you might be looking again, and sharing your thanks will encourage your contacts to help next time.

Chapter Wrap-Up

Building a network is something you must keep pursuing through hard work. A strong network is a key component in creating a family-friendly work arrangement. You will use your network in your search, whether you are looking to move to a new position within your company, or for a new position with a new company. Further, if you choose to go out on your own and start your own business, a good network can help you get your idea off the ground.

Resources

Books

The Art of the Business Lunch: Building Relationships Between 12 and 2 by Robin Jay (Career Press, 2006).

SuperNetworking; Reach the Right People, Build Your Career Network, and Land Your Dream Job— Now! by Michael Salmon (Career Press, 2003).

Websites

LinkedIn: *www.linkedin.com*
A free online networking organization that allows you to organize your contacts, find lost contacts, and make new contacts.

Executive Moms: *www.executivemoms.com*
Executive Moms provides women who are mothers and professionals with the networking, support, and unique resources to help them thrive in both roles. Membership is free.

Business and Professional Women: www.*bpwusa.org*
Provides advancement resources, worklife strategies, and personal and professional connections.

Job Hunt: *www.job-hunt.org*
Online job search site that includes networking resources, including a directory of professional associations and a directory of company alumni groups.

National Association of Female Executives: *www.nafe.com*
Provides resources and networking opportunities for professional women. It also provides a list of top companies for female executives.

Working Women: *www.womenworking.com*
Provides profiles of women who are movers and shakers in their fields, a list of Power Contacts, a lively Message Board, and more.

Chapter

13

Searching for Family-Friendly Work

Typically, a job search can be lot of work, but finding a family-friendly job takes even more effort. Unfortunately, job opportunities that welcome parents seeking a work-and-family balance are not yet abundant. Therefore, most of the work in securing a family-friendly job involves identifying potential opportunities. To accomplish this, you must take a targeted search approach.

Many search strategies will help you identify a family-friendly opportunity. Here, I will focus on a few that I believe are the most effective. Your best bet is networking and making personal contact. Researching companies that potentially have family-friendly benefits and policies will also uncover specific companies to target in your search. The Internet also provides many opportunities to find family-friendly work, and finally, you may want to call on a professional recruiter for assistance.

Why Networking Works

Few family-friendly opportunities exist because most managers find it easier to manage traditional schedules. However, many times a particular job or manager may be flexible enough to accommodate an alternate schedule. A referral from a current employee often quickly fills these limited opportunities; it just makes sense. Running a newspaper or other advertisement can cost a company thousands of dollars. Employee referrals are quicker, cheaper, and come with a solid reference. In fact, many companies encourage employees to refer potential new employees by offering monetary bonus payments for a referral.

Networking for a family-friendly job works for several reasons. A network contact can help you find out if a company is truly family-friendly, or at least if certain managers will accommodate an alternate schedule. Further, network contacts may know of companies looking for new employees before the company begins advertising openings. In fact, sometimes a company will even create a job for a good candidate referred to the company.

For example, Shelly was a successful graphic designer before she had children and decided to stay home. After a few years, Shelly wanted to start making a little money so she put the word out to her network about her search for work opportunities. A contact at a local product manufacturer forwarded her resume to the company's graphics department. With a big new project and a quick deadline ahead, the department manager sub-contracted Shelly to do some graphics work for a new product launch. After Shelly successfully met this challenge, the department manager continued to offer her work on a monthly basis. This opportunity worked well for Shelly, allowing her to generate income while continuing to stay at home. She ultimately created a position for herself that the company never would have advertised.

Networking can help you secure a position that meets your needs, and it happens all of the time. My dentist tells me of numerous job connections he has orchestrated between his patients. Successful networking requires a structured approach. Chapter 12 laid out the process of building and expanding your network. To use your network to find a job, you now need to put your network to work.

Using your network to find a job

Once you have identified some targeted information about the type of opportunity you want, notify your network. You can accomplish this easily by using personalized e-mail and/or a letter. Do not send a mass distribution e-mail or unpersonalized letter, as they will likely be discarded. In your message, share information about your search for a new opportunity. Provide details about your search and your need for flexibility. In addition, provide the names of some of the companies you want to target.

Sample E-mail Network Announcement

To: Sue Q.

From: Jane F.

Subject: New Career Opportunity

Dear Sue,

As you may already know, I am in the process of confidentially searching for a new career opportunity. I am ready to take my 12 years of accounting experience to a new company where I can create a more flexible full-time work arrangement, allowing me to meet the needs of my family. I am particularly interested in making contact with ABC Consulting, Tri-state Industries, and Global International. If you have contacts at any of these companies, or any other company that could benefit from my experience, please let me know. Thank you for your continued support!

Jane

In addition to a personal e-mail message or letter, make sure you mention your search whenever possible. Mention it to the coffee shop cashier, your eye doctor, and all those other contacts you identified in Chapter 12. Notifying your network will help you uncover some of those hidden job opportunities.

Next, your job search should include active expansion of your network. Use the tactics described in Chapter 12 to grow your network. Whenever possible, target your network growth to identify contacts in companies where you want to work. Look for ways to identify network links to specific companies. You can use online tools such as the LinkedIn Website mentioned at the end of Chapter 12. Contact your college alumni office to see if they provide networking opportunities, or ways to identify fellow alums working at specific companies. Get creative in your search for the right contact.

Most importantly, don't get frustrated. Networking requires a lot of time and effort. It is not only time consuming, but it is also a long process. You can't go out and start networking and expect to come across a job opportunity right away. Networking can take months, or even years to uncover a job opportunity. That is why it is important to start now, regardless of your job search status.

Researching Potential Employers

You must conduct research to identify companies to contact directly, or at least target through networking. You must use this active approach because as mentioned earlier, most family-friendly job opportunities never make it to the newspaper or Internet. After employee referrals, companies tend to look for direct contacts because they also cost little compared to advertising or other recruiting strategies.

Where to Research Family-Friendly Companies

➥ Newspapers or magazine articles about companies in your area.

➥ Local business news.

➥ Companies actively promoting women.

➥ National lists recognizing family-friendly employers.

➥ Family-friendly award announcements.

➥ Local lists recognizing companies respected by their employees.

➥ Businesses located close to your home.

➥ Kid-friendly organizations.

So where to begin? First, look for articles about companies who have family-friendly practices. Go to your local library and ask the reference librarian to help you search the research databases to find articles. Several magazines and newspapers feature articles about companies that have family-friendly practices. Your research should try to identify companies that offer flexible schedules and the family-friendly benefits and policies you learned about in Chapters 8, 9, and 10.

Start regularly reading the business section of your local newspaper. Look for stories about happenings at local companies highlighting family-friendly practices. For example, you might find an article about a company opening an on-site daycare. In addition to the general news, look for the section that announces recent promotions and new hires at local companies. Often, you will identify companies worth checking out because they regularly promote women (see Chapter 6).

Next, consult lists that document companies with family-friendly practices, such as *Working Woman* magazine's "100 Best Companies," or *Fortune* magazine's "Best Companies to Work For." Many nonprofit organizations also recognize family-friendly workplaces. For example, the Families and Work Institute gives the Alfred P. Sloan Awards for Business Excellence in Workplace Flexibility. The Catalyst Award recognizes companies with innovative approaches for recognizing and developing female talent.

You may also find a local publication or organization that identifies family-friendly companies in your area. For example, in my community, the Employers Resource Council, a local employer services organization, publishes a list of the 99 top companies. Companies make the list by becoming an "employer of choice," meaning they have management practices and offer benefits similar to those that make a company family-friendly. Another example is Starting Point, a local nonprofit agency that provides childcare referrals. This organization recently published a list of local family-friendly organizations. An Internet search using the keywords "family-friendly work" or "top employer," along with the name of your city or nearest metropolitan area, will likely pull up similar award lists in your area. You may want to also contact your local Chamber of Commerce, as they are likely to know of any such published lists.

In addition to the library database, you can use the Internet to search for articles about family-friendly companies. Google.com can help you with your research with a tool they call Google Alerts. You can enter keywords and then receive daily lists of any articles published on the Internet that contain those keywords. For example, you could enter "family-friendly work" or "flexible work," and the name of your city or state. At the end of each day, you will receive an e-mail message from Google listing any articles published that day anywhere on the Internet with your keywords.

Take note of companies that you drive past frequently. Proximity is important for a family-friendly work arrangement. By losing commute time, you gain family time. Also, check out generally well-known companies in your area, even if you haven't heard about their family-friendly policies. A company with a successful reputation will likely have positive management practices in place that often coincide with a family-friendly work environment.

Consider checking out organizations that work with kids or create products for kids. For example, nonprofit agencies that provide services for children or families will more likely understand the challenges that working parents face. On the for-profit side, companies that make products for kids, kid-centered restaurants, or other entertainment venues may be more understanding of child-related concerns. For example, Laura recently found a part-time position selling advertisements for a parent's magazine. A childcare conflict left her in a bind for the job interview. But her future boss welcomed her youngest daughter to join them for their initial meeting.

Once you have created a list of targeted companies, you must conduct further research to figure out the best way to contact the company. Check in with your network to see if you can identify a contact. Your resume will get more attention accompanied by a letter opening with "Your friend Bob suggested I contact you." Visit the company Website to see if the company posts job opportunities or a contact name. Avoid sending your resume to the company with a "Dear Sir or Madam" salutation. Your resume will receive more attention when directed to a specific person. If you do not identify a contact through your network or the Website, call the company directly. Ask the receptionist the name of the Human Resource Manager or Recruiter. Or ask for the name of the manager in the department to which you plan to send your resume.

Tapping the World Wide Web

Access to the Internet provides another place where we have an advantage over our predecessors in the family-friendly job search process. Throughout this book I reference many Websites helping parents balance work and family. These sites often have job posting boards or feature articles and other information about working parents who have found success identifying an alternative work arrangement.

You can also build your network virtually by joining discussion boards focusing on the needs of working parents. Active involvement in online discussions can help you build relationships with other parents who can share valuable advice with you in your job search. They can also become valuable networking contacts to help you identify potential opportunities. Online relationship building can be more time efficient than other forms of networking. You can also reach across geographic barriers for a search outside of your current geographic location.

You should also regularly search traditional job boards such as Monster, Hotjobs, Careerbuilder, or Craig's List. Many of these job career boards have extensive search options that allow you to type in keywords to search for family-friendly jobs; you may look for part-time jobs or do a keyword search. You should also keep an eye on posted full-time jobs that might lead to an alternate work schedule. If a company posts a job of interest to you, do some research on the company to see if the company supports family-friendly work.

Keyword Search Words

- ➥ Flexible.
- ➥ Nontraditional.
- ➥ Compressed workweek.
- ➥ Job share.
- ➥ Alternate schedule.
- ➥ Family-friendly.

In addition, you can use the Internet to explore the websites of various companies to determine if they are family-friendly. You can narrow down the company list that you identified in your research through some careful checking of a company Websites. Read about the company and get a feel for the company's culture by thoroughly exploring all parts of the Website. Look on the employment page for benefit listings to see if the company offers any family-friendly benefits discussed in Chapter 10. Check job postings for any part-time or alternate work schedules.

Using a Job Search Firm

Many companies hire third-party recruiters to help fill certain positions. These companies, often referred to as job search firms or headhunters, assist other companies in finding candidates for difficult to fill positions. Some firms actually specialize in helping candidates looking for more flexible work opportunities. These specialty firms can be useful, particularly when looking for a temporary assignment.

Traditional temporary employment agencies can also help you find a family-friendly work arrangement. Some agencies will put you on short-term assignments to meet your family needs. For example, an agency could put you on a one-week assignment, once each month. Or you could work on short-term assignments, but only while your children are in school. Assignments through a temporary agency allow you to work short stints at a time, without getting stigmatized as a "job-hopper."

Working with a job search firm has pros and cons; they do a lot of the work for you in trying to find a good job match. Often, they are aware of positions that exist in companies that may not be advertised elsewhere. However, not all companies want to work with a search firm to fill positions. This is an expensive search option for companies, who often pay fees equivalent to 25 to 35 percent of the new hire's first year of salary.

If you decide to work with a job search firm, here are a few tips:

➱ Do not pay a fee! The company hiring you should pay the fee to the firm. While some reputable firms do charge a fee to applicants, most do not. Plenty of options exist with firms whose fees are paid by the hiring company.

- ✏ Check the Better Business Bureau to make sure the firm you want to work with does not have any complaints against them.

- ✏ Make sure that you have plenty of opportunities to talk to your potential boss and other company employees. Treat this as any other opportunity and do a complete scan for a family-friendly environment.

- ✏ Remember, the firm only gets paid if you take the job. The recruiter at the search firm may be very persuasive and try to get you to take a job you don't want. If you do not want a job, do not take it.

- ✏ Be honest with the firm about what you want. Don't waste everyone's time interviewing for a position that you know you won't take.

It will take some effort to find job search firms that will help you search for a flexible opportunity. A couple of examples are listed at the end of the chapter, but others may exist in your local area. Search local Internet directories, or tap into your network to identify reputable firms to contact.

Final Job Search Thoughts

In addition to your targeted search, you should also continue to review weekly job advertisements in your local newspaper. While a company may not advertise flexible options, you might still find a job looking for your exact skill set. If so, a possibility exists that once you get in front of the hiring manager and convince him or her that you are the best candidate, a request for an alternate work arrangement might be considered. Chapters 14, 15, and 16 further discuss negotiation strategies during and after the job search process. You may also find that you must take a job and work a traditional schedule awhile before seeking a flexible schedule.

You may be fortunate to know of someone else in your field also looking for a family-friendly job. Consider uniting and conducting a search together to find a job share arrangement for an existing full-time job. This will take some extra work to identify a company welcoming to such an arrangement. Be prepared for some surprised and cool receptions, but if you have a good skill set to offer, you may convince the right company to give you an opportunity.

Chapter Wrap-Up

Pursuing a family-friendly work arrangement requires hard work. Some job-search experts suggest that you can estimate how long a job search will take based upon how much money you expect to make (roughly a one-month search for every $10,000 you expect to make, so it should take you about six months to find a job that pays $60,000 a year). You will need to add on a few more months if you want something family-friendly. Don't get discouraged! Remember the reason(s) behind your search.

Resources

Targeted Career Search Books

Internet Job Search Almanac edited by Robert Kehn (Adams Media, 2002).

Women for Hire: The Ultimate Guide to Getting a Job by Tory Johnson, Robyn Freedman Spizman, and Lindsey Pollak (Penguin Putnam, 2002).

Conducting Research

Best Workplaces for Commuters: *www.bwc.gov/campaign/index.htm*

Highlights workplaces with innovative ideas to limit traffic gridlock and poor air quality. It is a good source for a flexible work search because they feature companies that offer options such as compressed workweeks and tele-work.

Blue Suit Mom: *www.bluesuitmom.com*

Includes jobs database, articles, and discussion boards.

Craigslist: *www.craigslist.org*

Includes job postings, featuring many part-time and telecommuting opportunities.

Google Alerts: *www.google.com/alerts*

Allows you to get notifications of articles published anywhere on the Internet based on keywords you enter.

The Great Places to Work Institute: *www.greatplacestowork.com*

Compiles a list of best companies to work at. Can search the list by geographic area.

Independent Homeworkers Alliance: *www.homeworkers.org*

Telecommuting resource center that provides job leads on potential work-at-home opportunities.

The Riley Guide: *www.rileyguide.com*

Provides numerous resources and advice for an online job search. Will help you conduct research and find job postings.

Women Work!: *www.womenwork.org/resources/jobfinder.htm*

Job Board sponsored by The National Network for Women's Employment.

The Flexibility Alliance: *www.flexibilityalliance.org*

A nonprofit organization that supports professionals in creating flexible careers and companies in attracting and retaining talent through flexibility. Provides information on companies committed to providing flexible work options to parents.

Search Firms Specializing in Flexible Work

Flexible Resources, Inc.: *www.flexibleresources.com*

A search firm that specializes in placing individuals in flexible work arrangements such as part-time, job-sharing, and contract work.

Mom Corps: *www.momcorps.com*

Mom Corps is a matchmaker between companies looking to recruit and retain top talent and experienced professionals looking for flexibility.

Chapter 14

Getting the Job

After you identify an opportunity, you must next convince the hiring manager that he or she should hire you. Because only limited family-friendly opportunities exist, you must put your best foot forward in the hiring process. Hiring typically involves several steps, all essentially aimed at eliminating you from the process. The company must narrow down the applicant pool to just a few applicants and then the final candidate. You must survive the weeding out process by submitting a perfect resume and nailing the interview.

Your Resume

Every career-search expert recommends the perfect resume. Yet, many applicants continue to send poorly written resumes full of errors. I spent several years as a recruiter, and continue to review resumes for clients in my consulting business. I estimate that one out of every five resumes I see contains errors. Even minor errors in your resume create a short cut to the trash pile. Further, many applicants submit poorly structured resumes that include irrelevant information. Failing to effectively communicate your qualifications will also speed you along the path to the trash pile. However, the following tips will get you started in the right direction.

Proofread, proofread, proofread

I have personally thrown at least a hundred resumes in the trash due to typos. Yes, minor typing errors will get your resume discarded even if you have wonderful experience. A recruiter or hiring manager usually wants to screen resumes out quickly, and typos and other errors make it easy to say no. Your resume should represent your best work. If you make spelling or other errors on such an important document, the reader questions the quality of the other work you will produce. If you can't get this one document perfect, you probably won't pay too much attention to details on a daily basis.

Read and reread your resume. Try reading it bottom to top to specifically look for errors. Look for consistent use of punctuation. Do you have a period at the end of each bullet point? Check for consistent use of italics or bold. For example, if you italicize your job title for one job, use italics on the title for every job. Have several friends read it. Most importantly, don't rely upon your computer's spell-check function.

Spell Checker Poem

Eye halve a spelling chequer
It came with my pea sea
It plainly marques four my revue
Miss steaks eye kin knot sea.

Eye have run this poem threw it
I am shore your pleased two no
Its letter perfect awl the weigh
My chequer tolled me sew.

—Source unknown

Keep it brief

Unless you pursue an academic career, or have more than 20 years of experience, your resume should not exceed two pages. If possible, keep it to one page. In most situations, your resume gets five seconds or less of attention, particularly if you send it in response to an advertisement. With only a few seconds to look, the third or fourth page usually doesn't even get a glance.

You can edit your resume down by eliminating any information not relevant to the position. For example, if you apply for a position as an administrative assistant, a detailed description of your job waiting tables isn't that relevant. Just include a one line item about the irrelevant employment to account for the time. Include only relevant extra activities, awards, or memberships. Your recognition as the "Bowler of the Year" at your local alley might be important to you, but a potential employer probably does not care.

About time at home

If you left the workforce for any period of time to raise your children, you must address that time on your resume. Many hesitate in mentioning time home with children because they think that the company may not respect the decision to stay home. Let me tell you, a gap on your resume does you more harm. Without an explanation, the hiring manager wonders if you just couldn't find a job, or if you were perhaps otherwise unavailable to work (such as being in jail). Therefore, you must explain your time at home. As I've said before and I will say again, a company that skips over you because you spent some time at home with your children most likely is not a family-friendly company. Chapter 20 provides some suggestions on how to write this section of your resume.

Applying online

Some companies ask you to complete an online application instead of submitting a resume. You need to take the same careful approach to filling out an online application as you do writing your resume. Your online application goes directly to a recruiter or hiring manager who screens the application the same way he or she would screen your resume. Misspellings, poor grammar, and incomplete sections will reflect poorly on you.

If you can upload your resume to the Website, remember that word-processing software often changes the format of a document depending on the version of the software. As a result, when the hiring manager at the company opens your resume, your perfectly formatted resume may be a mess. I suggest converting your resume document into an Adobe (.pdf) file so that the format looks exactly as you created it.

Online applications typically go through an electronic screening process to scan for key words or experiences. For example, if the position requires a bachelor's degree, the system will screen out any applications without a bachelor's degree listed. You must carefully read the job posting of interest to you. Pick out keywords to include in your experience listing. For example, if the position requires a lot of client contact and you have client contact experience, make sure you use the term "client contact" somewhere in your application. The more keywords included, the more likely your application will make it to the next round.

Initiating Contact

After you have your resume ready to go, you need to get it to the right person. How you approach this depends on how you learned about the opportunity. If responding to an advertisement, follow the directions listed. E-mail your resume or send it via the postal service, whatever they ask you to do. If the advertisement states "no phone calls;" do not call.

Whether you send via e-mail or the postal service, you should include a cover letter. The cover letter should be a simple, brief letter including three parts. The first paragraph indicates the position you want and how you became aware of the opportunity. If someone referred you to the company, let the hiring manager know that. The first sentence of your cover letter should say, "Joe Smith suggested I contact you." Your letter will more likely be read if the contact knows who sent you. The second paragraph should briefly highlight the experiences you have that make you an ideal candidate for the position. The final paragraph thanks the reader for his or her time and consideration and states that you will be in touch with them to schedule an interview.

If you respond to an advertisement using e-mail, only send your resume as an attachment if told to do so. Otherwise, include your resume in the body of your e-mail. Concerns with viruses lead many to not open attachments. Also, do not include your cover letter as a separate attachment. Just type your cover letter as the body of your e-mail.

If possible, send your resume directly to the hiring manager. However, you must be respectful to the human resources (HR) representative if the company has one. Many career-search guides will tell you to circumvent HR, because HR generally intends to screen you out. However, you do not know what kind of relationship the HR person has with the hiring manager. If they have a good relationship, then disrespect to the HR manager will eliminate you from consideration. As a former HR manager, I developed a mutually beneficial relationship with the managers I supported. They counted on me to know their business and to save them time by forwarding only qualified applicants to them. If job applicants purposely ignored my calls and called the hiring manager directly, they were quickly labeled as difficult to work with and eliminated from the process.

If you intend to negotiate a regular full-time position into an alternate work arrangement, do not reference your need for a flexible work arrangement in your cover letter. Focus on the opportunity,

> ## Preparing for the Interview
>
> ✎ Research the company.
> ✎ Prepare your responses.
> ✎ Practice responding to questions.
> ✎ Prepare questions to ask.

and more specifically, the skills and abilities you bring to the job. You hold the power in the negotiation process when you have something the company wants. At this early stage in the process, they don't know what you have to offer and will not be interested in negotiating. Wait until you have established yourself as the best candidate for the job and then bring up your proposal for alternate work. Chapters 15 and 16 further discuss the negotiation process.

The Interview

Whether you have found an elusive flexible work opportunity, or a job that you will later negotiate into an alternate arrangement, you must first get through the interview process. Thorough preparation and polished responses in the interview will help you succeed. The following tips will get you started on developing this essential skill.

Do your homework

Research and find out everything you can about the company and the position. Start with the company's Website if it has one. Look for information on the history of the company, investor relation information, and recent news. Check out the leaders of the company. If you interview with a public company, request an annual report and read about past company performance as well as future strategic directions. Go to the library and do some research to find recent news articles about the company. Look for new products the company has developed, new businesses they have acquired, or if they have a new competitor. Your research will prepare you to ask questions about the company in the interview.

Have your responses ready

Many people assume they can just walk in, answer questions, and be successful with the interview; however, with just a little effort, you can increase your odds for success in the interview process. Get a book about interviewing, and read it thoroughly. Practice responses to common interviewing questions.

Many companies use the behavioral interview approach. Behavioral interviews seek to identify your ability to do the job by asking for examples of how you have performed certain tasks in the past. In a behavioral interview, you will likely hear questions starting with "Tell me about a time when..." or "Give me an example of...."

To prepare for a behavioral interview, make a list of good stories you can tell to illustrate your abilities that the position requires. Does the position require a good problem solver? Think of a time you solved a problem at work (or at home) and write down the situation. Does the position require multi-tasking? Think of a day that your multi-tasking helped you finish a project.

Do some research to determine what skills, abilities, or experiences the interviewer might ask you about to determine what kind of stories you'll need. If you have a job description or advertisement for the position, you have a good start. You may have also uncovered some specifics about what you need if you conducted informational interviews. The U.S. Department of Labor also maintains a thorough database of job titles that lists the required knowledge, skills, and abilities for thousands of positions (see link at the end of the chapter).

Interviewees often find responding to behavioral interview questions challenging. Often a candidate goes on and on telling a story but doesn't really get to the point, or tells too little of the story to demonstrate his or her capabilities. You want to share information about the situation that demonstrates your ability by explaining specifically what you did in the situation, and how your employer benefited. I suggest using the "STAR" response.

The STAR Response to Behavioral Interview Questions

Example question:

Tell me about a time when you had to resolve an issue with a difficult customer.

Your response:

☞ **"S"=Situation:** Here you provide the context for the story.

"In my last job I was a customer service representative at a bank and handled phone calls from customers with questions about their accounts."

☞ **"T"=Task:** Or problem with which you were faced.

"One time a very angry customer called upset because he had an extra service charge on his account. He demanded that I connect him to a supervisor."

☞ **"A"=Action:** What you specifically did to solve the problem.

"I told him I could understand his frustration, and that I thought I could help him. He still demanded to speak to a supervisor, so I suggested that he give me his account information, that way I could pull up his account and then still let him speak to a supervisor. I explained that the supervisor would need me to explain the problem. He calmed down and gave me the account number. I pulled it up and quickly found the error, I told him what had happened and that I could reverse the charges, and he could immediately see the update on his online account."

✏ **"R"=Result:** How your actions benefited the company.

"I did not have to get a supervisor to speak with him. He pulled up the account and was surprised at first that I was able to fix it so quickly. He thanked me and apologized for being so brisk. Actually, he even gave me high marks on the follow-up survey my company sends out."

Keep in mind, however, that not all interviewers have good interviewing skills. In fact, you will more likely face an inexperienced and untrained interviewer than a skillful and trained interviewer. Listen attentively at all times during the interview process. If the interviewer tends to talk a lot, and therefore asks few questions, look for opportunities to share information.

Always ask questions at the end of the interview. If you say you have no questions, you leave an impression of disinterest. Asking questions allows you to do some digging and find out more about the company. If you have no indication on the family friendliness of the company, you can ask questions to probe. But don't only focus on the family-friendly aspect of the company. Ask questions about the job responsibilities, opportunities for growth, and success. You can also ask the interviewer questions about his or her job and personal experience with the company.

Be prepared to talk about your family

You must consider how you want to talk about your family. Remember that an employer should not ask you about your personal life or your childcare arrangements; but you may want to prepare yourself to mention the fact that you do have a family who you still want to see after you get the job. However, don't cross the fine line between mentioning your family and overdoing it.

If family does come up, you can gain some insight on whether or not the company will be family-friendly. My friend Kerry told me that an interviewer asked her if she was ready to return to work after being home with her kids for a few years. She said she was, and that she would be a committed employee. But in all fairness, she told them she did have three small children, and while she had a solid childcare plan in place, there may be occasions when she would need to handle an emergency. She took this as an opportunity to ask about the company's flexibility. She thinks that this discussion may have cost her the job, but she said she wouldn't want to work anywhere that would not allow her to meet her children's needs.

Sample Questions About Family-Friendly

- ✐ What is a typical day here like?
- ✐ What do you like most about working here?
- ✐ How would you describe the company culture?
- ✐ What is the average tenure of your employees? (Or, do you have many long-term employees?)
- ✐ Are there any benefits to help support working parents?

The follow-up

Even though every career advice book you will ever read will tell you to send a thank-you note, you would be surprised at how few people follow that guideline. I have recruited individuals for many years. I have hired more than 500 employees, and while I haven't kept track, I probably have conducted more than 2,000 interviews. In that time, I estimate I have received maybe 100 thank-you notes. And it does matter, especially if two candidates have similar qualifications. All else equal, the person who sends the thank-you note has an advantage because he or she has expressed a sincere interest in the position.

Beyond the thank-you note, you can call to followup, but don't become too aggressive. At the conclusion of the interview, state your interest in the position and ask for a reasonable time frame for a decision. After that time has passed, make a call to check in on the position. However, if you start calling the manager or recruiter too often, it can quickly become a turn-off. Overly aggressive candidates become a nuisance, and you will likely lose your opportunity to get the position even if you do have good qualifications.

Chapter Wrap-Up

Whether you apply for a specific family-friendly opportunity, or apply to the perfect opportunity to negotiate into a family-friendly arrangement, you must put your best foot forward in the process. If your resume goes directly to the trash, you have no opportunity to discuss the position in person. Further, if you blow the interview, you can't negotiate the family-friendly work arrangement.

Resources

Books

The Career Change Resume by Karen Hofferber and Kim Isaacs (McGraw Hill, 2003).

Expert Resumes for People Returning to Work by Wendy S. Enelow and Louise M. Kursmark (Jist Publishing, 2003).

Going Back to Work: A Survival Guide for Comeback Moms by Mary W. Quigley and Loretta E. Kaufman (St. Martin's Griffin, 2004).

No-Nonsense Resumes: The Essential Guide to Creating Attention-Grabbing Resumes That Get Interviews and Job Offers by Wendy S. Enelow and Arnold G. Boldt (Career Press, 2006).

Winning Job Interviews: Reduce Interview Anxiety/Out prepare the Other Candidates/Land the Job You Love by Dr. Paul Powers (Career Press, 2004).

Job Search Boards With Advice

Blue Suit Mom: *www.bluesuitmom.com*

CareerBuilder: *www.careerbuilder.com*

Moms Resumes: *www.momsresumes.com*

Monster: *www.monster.com*

Yummy Mummy Careers: *www.yummymummycareers.com*

Department of Labor

Occupational Information Network: *http://online.onetcenter.org*

Chapter

15

Asking for
Flexibility in
Your Current
Job

The best opportunity for family-friendly work exists with your current employer. If a company already has confidence in your capabilities, the company will more likely grant your request. When I asked Kevin, who worked part-time after his first child was born, how he negotiated a part-time arrangement with his employer, he told me "I just asked." He had been with the small family-owned business for several years, and the owners knew he would work out a way to make sure he succeeded.

A company takes a risk when approving an alternate work arrangement. It often requires more work on behalf of management, and even peers in many situations. However, the payoffs for the company can be immense. The company benefits from the employee's increased commitment to the job and increased loyalty to the company. In many situations, workers in alternate work arrangements actually increase their productivity. The decision to take that risky approach will more likely happen if the company knows the employee's performance and has confidence that the risk will payoff.

However, an alternate arrangement may be a challenge if no other employees at the company work in such arrangements. Further, even if others at your company work in alternate arrangements, it does not mean that your manager will grant your request. If your company already has flexible work arrangements in place, then you have an advantage in the negotiating process. However, a company reserves the right to apply such policies differently for different people, as long as they can claim business reasons and not discriminatory reasons for the decision.

So, how do you approach requesting an alternate work arrangement? Well, as Kevin suggests, you just ask. But before you ask, make sure you have done your research and have your proposal ready to go. You don't want to meet your boss's enthusiasm to consider your idea with "I will write you a proposal." You want to capitalize on that enthusiasm and have the proposal ready to go. Here I will address the steps you must take to get prepared, and in Chapter 16 you will learn how to write and deliver the proposal.

Evaluating if Flexibility Will Work for Your Job

Consider the nature of your job and responsibilities as you begin to evaluate your options. Review some of the characteristics of a family-friendly job discussed in Chapter 7. If your current job does not hold any of these characteristics, then consider if you might be able to find a new job at your current company. You can more easily negotiate a flexible work arrangement in a new job at your current company than a new job at a new company.

You could also look for an opportunity to create a new flexible job at your company. For example, Robin worked in the records management department of a hospital and was denied her first request to transition her full-time supervisory role into a part-time position. The hospital needed someone there every day to handle supervisory responsibilities. However, Robin knew of several tasks and responsibilities in her department that were not getting done because of the supervisors' heavy workloads, so she proposed a new part-time position to handle those tasks. Her request was granted.

You must also consider what will happen if your company denies your request. You may know that you will face a bumpy road to an alternate work arrangement. In fact, in some cases just requesting an alternate work arrangement will make your boss think that you no longer feel committed to your job. If you suspect this might be the case, you must be ready to search outside of your company if you cannot get the arrangement you want. If you really want this change, you have to commit to getting it, which might mean moving on to a new company in the end.

Your Approach

Once you have committed yourself to requesting an alternate arrangement, you must begin to prepare to write your proposal. You must be informed and prepared to successfully negotiate your proposed work arrangement. To start your preparation, you must consider your approach to your request as thoughtfully as you consider the type of arrangement that you want.

The authors of the legendary negotiating guide *Getting to Yes*, recommend focusing on interests and mutual gain instead of positions in the negotiation process. When each side takes a position, the focus becomes give and take, and you often do not arrive at the optimal arrangement. Further, positional negotiating often leads to negative relationships. For example, you focus on your position when you focus your preparation on the fact that you need a flexible work arrangement to meet your family's needs. Your boss may hold the position that he or she wants you to work standard hours. The negotiation process becomes a battle where only one of you wins. It might work out, but you will more likely jeopardize your relationship with your boss in the process.

Instead, you should focus on interests and mutual gain. You have an interest in your work becoming more compatible with your family life while still advancing your career. Your boss has interest in ensuring that the company succeeds. You must work to create an arrangement that allows mutual gain. That is, an arrangement that allows you to meet your family obligations without sacrificing your career and helps support your boss's pursuit of company success.

Your interests

In Chapter 2, I reviewed the importance of determining what you really need from a flexibility perspective. Focus on the priorities that you established in determining what kind of arrangement will work for you. Keep in mind your career interests as well as your family interests. You want to create a work situation that allows you to meet both.

Start by listing your priorities in the negotiation process. Do you need just a little more flexibility, or to reduce your hours? How will this new arrangement help you improve your performance? Will you be less distracted by home obligations so you can focus better? Will you need to commute less so you can save money, making it more financially viable to work? Will you feel more positive about your job because it does not conflict with your home life?

Your company's interests

Next, you must consider your company's interests. You must create the business case for your alternative arrangement. To figure this out, you must do some research to determine how to support your request from the company's perspective. How will your company benefit from you working in an alternate work arrangement?

First, consider your boss's priorities. How does management measure his or her performance? Does he or she have specific production goals to meet? Does the company measure customer satisfaction? What does your boss want from you? What has your boss measured your performance by in the past?

Also, consider current activities at your company. Is the company growing, or cutting back? Is the company developing new products, or just maintaining the status quo? Understanding your company's goals and future direction will help you determine your company's interests.

Finally, does your company have a sense of social responsibility? A company acts in a socially responsible manner when the company takes steps in the best interest of the local community and society in general. Alternate work schedules have many benefits to the community. For example, approving alternate work schedules supports the community by supporting families and working in cooperation with local school systems. Alternate work arrangements can also support the community by supporting the environment through cutting down on pollution if your schedule means that you have less or no commuting.

Creating mutual gain

Based on your analysis of both your own interests and your company's interests, you must start to articulate how your proposed arrangement creates mutual gain. Ultimately you want to present your proposal as a solution. Make a list of the ways in which the new arrangement will make you a more productive employee. Try to quantify the effects of your boss granting your alternate work arrangement request.

Some facts to support your request

According to the 2002 National Study of the Changing Workforce by the Families and Work Institute, flexible work arrangements create:

✎ Higher levels of job satisfaction.

✎ Increased commitment to the employer.

✎ Longer retention.

✎ Less interference between job and family life.

✎ Better mental health.

For example, your personal benefit of less stress and more balance will benefit your company. If you worry less about home, you can concentrate on your work and be a more effective employee. Lower stress levels will help you be more productive. Also, because alternate work arrangements do not readily exist elsewhere, your company approving your request will build your loyalty to the company, reducing, or better yet, eliminating the possibility that you will leave. Companies lose a lot of money due to turnover, so this represents a potential cost savings.

What other advantages will your alternate arrangement provide for your company? For example, if you come into work earlier, you may be able to work more productively due to less distraction. Many years ago I worked in a flexible arrangement at a bank while I was completing my master's degree. My university only offered a particular class at 4 in the afternoon two days a week. On those two days, I worked from 6:30 a.m. until 3:30 p.m. Before 8 a.m. when everyone else arrived at the office, I accomplished an extraordinary amount of work. Here are some other ways you may become more productive in an alternate schedule:

✎ If your recommendation includes working from home, consider how much of a cost savings this could provide your employer. Could you completely eliminate your need for workspace at your company? Could you share your space with someone else?

✎ Your reduction in hours could provide more opportunity for someone else in the company. You could, for example, delegate some of your duties to a less senior employee who would not otherwise be able to get such experience.

✏ A job share arrangement could provide better coverage of a particular job. If you covered for each other during illness or other absences, your arrangement could provide continuous job coverage for a critical position in a company.

✏ You could better service customers if you work alternate hours. For example, if your office typically opens at 8 a.m. and you start opening it at 7 a.m., customers get the benefit of an extra hour of customer service.

These are only a few examples of how your alternate arrangement could create mutual gain for you and your company. Sit down with the list of your interests and your company's interests and brainstorm ideas on how to achieve mutual gain. Solicit ideas from friends and colleagues. Find research on companies that have been successful in working with alternate work schedules. Find examples of companies with successful programs, such as those on the *Working Mother* magazine's list. Look for publications or resources in your particular industry on alternate work schedules.

Working Out the Details

After you have determined the work arrangement that you will request, and how that arrangement will create mutual gain, consider what you need to have in place to make it work. For example, you can't request a job share until you have identified a job share partner. You also need to also prepare yourself to respond to any concerns your boss might have with your request.

Consider any challenges your new arrangement will create and how to address those challenges. For example, if you request a reduced schedule, who will handle your excess workload? Could any of your responsibilities or duties be eliminated? Can you change your work to reduce your workload?

If you want an alternate full-time schedule or a part-time schedule, do you foresee any concerns about someone needing you while you are not at the office? How available will you be in your off hours? Will you only check e-mail, or will you welcome calls to your home? Or will you not be available at all?

Be prepared to respond to concerns. Does your job involve travel? If so, how will you handle it? What happens when meetings take place on your off days? What about busy times when people must work overtime? The more objections you address in your proposal, the more likely your company will accept the proposal.

Consider what you can offer to make the arrangement more attractive to your company. For example, if your company faces some tough times, then you might want to figure out how to present your request to meet the financial concerns. Obviously cutting back your hours will save the company money. Further, if you can get benefits such as health insurance coverage elsewhere (such as through your spouse), consider offering to do so.

As you consider your proposal, make sure you do not commit to more than you can do. If fact, you should commit to do a little less than you plan to do. It is far better to exceed expectations than to fall short. Further, many parents taking on alternate schedules over-commit and end up taking a cut in pay to do the same amount of work.

Compensation concerns

If you continue working full-time hours, your salary and benefits should remain the same. If your employer suggests a reduction in pay if you work at home or take on a compressed workweek or some other full-time schedule, you should not accept it. If you continue to produce the same amount of work, your should receive the same pay. However, if your proposal involves a reduction in hours, you will, most likely, also take a reduction in pay as discussed in Chapter 9 and sometimes a reduction in benefits as discussed in Chapter 10.

If you rely on your company's benefits, you must do some research to determine how your reduction in schedule will affect your eligibility to receive benefits. For example, if you need to maintain your health insurance benefits, you need to find out the minimum weekly hours you must work to keep them.

Beyond pay and benefits, you must also consider your paid time off allotment. Your paid time off includes vacation days, sick days, and personal days or PTO (paid time off) days. The structure of this benefit will likely be affected by an alternate work schedule, whether you work full-time or part-time. For example, if you shift to a four-day compressed workweek and you normally receive 10 vacation days, your employer will probably not give you 10, 10-hour vacation days. To keep your vacation time the same (40 hours) you can request eight, 10-hour vacation days.

If you work a varied schedule, the paid time off calculation becomes more complex. For example, you face a dilemma if you request a new schedule to work full-time each week, two eight-hour days, and two 12-hour days. Again, you should convert your time-off allowance to the equivalent of your current allowance. In this case I suggest keeping the 10-day allowance of vacation, but count your 12-hour days as 1 1/2 vacation days when you take them.

If you cut back your hours, you should pro-rate your paid time-off allowance. For example, if you transition from 40 hours to 20 hours each week, you should reduce your time-off allowance by half. For part-timers, it is easiest to track your time off by the hour.

Building Relationships

As you start researching and writing your proposal, you should also begin to align allies to support you. You obviously want your boss in your corner, so you should ensure that your performance exceeds expectations. You should continue working hard and not let your boss down, particularly during the few months before you bring up your proposal.

You may also want to consider building relationships with other parents in your company. Start an informal networking group and meet over lunch to discuss creative ways that your company can improve the life of working parents while improving the company's bottom line. Such support groups can give you a lot of advice in writing your proposal, particularly if some already worked in an alternate work arrangement. More importantly, they can provide you with moral support as you pursue your request.

Chapter Wrap-Up

If you enjoy your job and you enjoy your company, your current position offers your best bet for a family-friendly work arrangement. Your proven track record with the company will increase the likelihood that your company grants your request. If your company does not currently have anyone else working in an alternate work arrangement, then you will face challenges. However, do not use that as an excuse not to try. You must do your research and prepare to write a proposal that will secure the work arrangement you want.

Resources

Books

Getting to Yes by Roger Fisher, William Ury and Bruce Patton (Random House, 2003).

Websites Featuring Work and Family Research to Support Your Request

Center for Work-Life Policy: *www.worklifepolicy.org*

Undertakes research and works with employers to design, promote, and implement workplace policies that increase productivity and enhance personal/family well-being. Check "News Room" for free summaries of research.

Families and Work Institute: *www.familiesandwork.org/announce/workforce.html*

Provides research on the effects of flexible work and other family-friendly benefits in the workforce.

Sloan Work and Family Research Network: *http://wfnetwork.bc.edu*

A research network at Boston College to promote informed decision-making about work and family issues.

Chapter 16

Writing and Delivering Your Proposal

Once you have worked out the details of your ideal arrangement, you must write a proposal. You should have a written proposal ready to go before bringing up your request with your boss. The written proposal demonstrates that you have thoroughly thought out your plan, and it gives your boss a document to review carefully. Your boss may also need something to pass along to any others in the company who need to approve the arrangement. While your face-to-face meeting with your boss will be a pivotal part of this process, the written document will be your key selling tool.

Writing the Proposal

The tone of your proposal must focus on the mutual gain of your recommended arrangement. Your boss must focus on ensuring that the business unit he or she manages runs as efficiently and effectively as possible. Therefore, your proposal must focus on convincing your boss that the proposed arrangement reflects a good business decision.

The content and format of the proposal may vary based on your unique request. You should, however, present it in a type-written, professional manner. Take time to brush up on your writing skills and grammar to ensure you present an impeccable document. The following list describes all of the sections you should include.

✎ **Introduction.** The introduction provides a summary of your request. You should briefly state that the following proposal requests an alternate work arrangement and a general overview of your proposal.

✎ **Your proposed arrangement.** Provide an outline of the work arrangement you want. Which days will you work? What hours? Will any work be at home? You may want to include a graphic representation of your proposed workweek. This may look similar to a grid with your schedule of each workday outlined.

✎ **Work specifications.** This section outlines your plan to make your alternate arrangement successful. Here you will address how you will complete your work in this arrangement, your plan for transitioning work to others if necessary, and your plan to handle any other individuals affected by your recommended change. If you request a reduced-hour schedule or a compressed workweek, you should address your availability on your off days. Will you check e-mail? Can your boss or coworkers call you? If you will work from home, this section should address how you will keep in touch, when you will work in your office, and so on.

✎ **Contingency plans.** This section will address how you will handle any fluctuations in your workload. If the company has a sudden increase in business, how will you adjust your schedule? Also, indicate how you will handle any meetings or other events that occur on your off days.

➯ **Compensation.** If you will continue in a full-time position, indicate no changes in pay or benefits. If applicable, you should note any change in the structure of your paid time-off allowance. If you request a reduction in your hours, you need to address your suggested changes in pay, benefits, and paid time-off allowances.

➯ **Company's gain.** Highlight here your research on how this arrangement will benefit your company. Include outside research to support your points. Highlight all of the benefits you identified when reading Chapter 15.

➯ **Support resources.** In this section you must include any support or resources you need, for example, if you plan to do some work from home, any technology or other support you will need. If you decide that you can use your home computer, you may ask your employer to provide Internet access for you if needed.

➯ **Trial period.** Recommend a trial period to test the new arrangement. A trial period will help assure your employer that you will do what it takes to make the arrangement work. Further, it will indicate your willingness to change if the arrangement doesn't initially work.

➯ **Evaluation.** Finally, you must indicate how you will determine if the arrangement works. Will you look at productivity reports? Will both you and your boss sit down and discuss it? Will you collect responses from your customers? Your coworkers? At the end of the trial period and moving forward, how will you determine if your work arrangement is successful?

What not *to include in your proposal*

Your proposal should build the business case for your alternate work arrangement request. You must convince your employer that the business will benefit from granting your request. Your reasons for needing such an arrangement are irrelevant. Do not include a sad story about your stressful life and your inability to manage your children's needs. Many in your company likely face the same stresses as you do. Again, while a family-friendly company will often be sympathetic to your needs as a parent, you should instead focus on the benefits to your company. Also, do not threaten to leave if your boss does not accept your proposal. Doing so suggests that you will not negotiate and you will not be flexible with the company even if they accept your proposal.

The Delivery

Introduce your request in person. A written proposal just placed in your boss's mailbox will not receive the same priority as the personal delivery of your request. If you do not meet regularly with your boss, ask him or her to reserve a time for you to meet. Pay careful consideration to the timing of your request. The "perfect time" does not exist, however, you probably don't want to bring up your request immediately following a meeting when your boss announces a shortage of staff for an upcoming project. Also, avoid particular times of the week or month when you know your boss faces an important deadline or another source of stress. I also suggest holding off on your request if your company faces an acquisition or merger with another company, unless you think your proposal may offer a solution. For example, if lay-offs will likely occur, a request for a part-time schedule may prove a useful solution for the company.

At the meeting, introduce your request with confidence. Briefly share the details of the work arrangement you want, and then move quickly to emphasizing the benefits to the company. Explain that the proposal you have in hand provides complete details of your request, and ask him or her to review it. Then, request a follow-up meeting to discuss it in more detail.

Negotiating

Be prepared for a lukewarm response to your request. Very rarely will a manager quickly accept all of the terms of a request for an alternate work arrangement. You could receive a wide range of responses, from a flat out no to an enthusiastic embrace of your request. Most likely, you will get something in the middle.

If you've done your homework and your proposal has already addressed many potential concerns of your boss, then you might just have to answer some basic clarification questions to your request. When responding to questions, don't rush and answer too quickly. You don't want to promise something you can't deliver later.

Warm responses

Often, a manager may be open to granting your request, but will have some reservations. At this point, you must take the lead in easing any of his or her concerns. For example, if your boss has a concern that you won't be able to meet your customer's needs, remind him or her of the trial period you suggest. The trial period will allow you to collect feedback from the customers to provide evidence that their needs have been met.

Many managers will respond: "If I give you this schedule, then everyone else will request a similar schedule." Respond to this question carefully. Understand that your boss has a responsibility to treat everyone fairly. Your request may indeed spark other's interests in requesting an alternate schedule. Just because you asked first, does not mean that your boss must only consider your request. Some possible responses to this concern:

✏ If you have requested a reduced-hour schedule, remind your boss that not everyone can take the pay reduction that accompanies a reduced hour schedule.

✏ Ask your boss what concerns he or she has with more than one person having an alternate schedule. It may require a little bit more managing on his or her part, but keep in mind the promised payoff. You and others become more loyal employees with increased productivity.

✏ Emphasize the trial period for your request. Tell your boss that you can be the experiment for an alternate work arrangement. If it doesn't work out, he or she can deny future requests. If it does work out (which you will make sure it does), then he or she has reason to consider anyone else's request also.

A Flat Out No

If you get a flat out no, don't just walk away. A no response begins the negotiation stage. Use the following strategies to respond:

✏ Ask your boss for specific criticism of your proposal. Find out exactly what concerns he or she has with the proposal. Is it the number of hours you want to work? Is it your proposed work coverage? Does he or she think you won't be committed to your job? Find out what further information you need to provide by identifying the weaknesses in your request.

✏ If your boss already tried an alternate arrangement with another employee and it didn't work out, find out what happened. Ask your boss, or your peers for more details. What can you do differently?

✏ Find out if you were off the mark on his or her interests. Do the proposed benefits of the proposal not meet his or her needs? What is important? Point out how your success in this arrangement will reflect positively on both of you.

☞ Again, remind your boss of the trial period. By saying yes, he or she does not commit to a permanent arrangement.

☞ Consider aligning yourself with others who want flexibility as well. A group request for flexibility may carry more weight than your individual request.

☞ Ask for help from an ally in your company. Is there someone higher up in the organization that can help you work with your boss? Or do you have a good relationship with a former boss or other peer of your boss's that might be able to help you? Is there a Human Resource representative who can support you?

☞ If your boss claims that he or she can't approve such a request because it runs against company policy, ask if you can speak with higher-ups about changing company policy. Again, if others in your company are looking for flexibility in their work, band together to persuade your company to change the policy.

Ask again, and again, and again. Circumstances may change, or your boss may simply get worn down and decide to give it a shot. However, when you ask, change your approach. The same question will likely bring you the same answer. Take feedback from previous requests and respond to concerns. Do further research to bring more support for your request. Go back to the drawing board and start over.

Ultimately, however, at some point you may have to make the decision as to whether or not your request will ever be granted. If you have asked repeatedly and been denied, at some point it may not make sense to continue asking. If you have a manager set in his or her ways, then you may have to abandon hope in converting him or her and start looking for another opportunity.

What you can offer

If your boss has some concerns with your request, think creatively about options to respond to those concerns. The most common concerns include the quality and quantity of the work you will provide in your new arrangement. Think creatively of any alternative you can offer to help alleviate this concern. For example, if you request a part-time schedule, can you work an extra day at home to cover some work? If you want to work a compressed schedule, can you be on-call on your day off?

Consider scaling back your request to just a small change in your schedule. For example, if you want to work at home a few days each week, ask your boss if you could just try a few hours one day a week. After a trial period where you have demonstrated that your work quality and quantity hasn't been affected, you can try to negotiate for more.

What else can you offer in your negotiation process? What would create a benefit for the company? For example, if you receive bonuses from your company, offer to take time off instead of the monetary bonus. Or can you take on a responsibility that no one else wants if your boss grants your request? Think creatively about what you can offer.

Chapter Wrap-Up

A well-written proposal goes a long way to convince your boss that your proposed arrangement represents a good business decision. The more professional and complete your proposal, the more difficult you make it for your boss to deny your request. By doing your research and presenting your idea in a well-thought out manner, you have given yourself an advantage in the process. And remember, the written proposal just starts the process. After you have delivered the proposal, be prepared to begin negotiating.

Resources

Books

The Elements of Style by William Strunk Jr. and E. B. White (Longman, 1999).

How to Win Any Negotiation by Robert Mayer (Career Press, 2006).

Successful Negotiation Strategies for Women by Wendy Keller (Career Press, 2006).

Websites

Work Options: *www.workoptions.com*

Offers a fill-in-the-blank proposal template to help working mothers and others to get their boss to say "yes" to a flexible work arrangement request.

Part

IV

After
Your
Search

Chapter

17

Making It
Work Day
to Day

Making your family-friendly arrangement work requires an ongoing effort. The option to work an alternate schedule represents a benefit, not an entitlement. You should treat the arrangement with respect and make sure you don't take advantage of the opportunity. Unless you have a signed contract with company, the company has no obligation to continue to support your alternate work arrangement. With that in mind, you can take steps to make sure your arrangement succeeds.

Making Your Family-Friendly Work a Success

- ✎ Be firm, but flexible.
- ✎ Communicate effectively.
- ✎ Take control of your time.
- ✎ Work together.
- ✎ Involve your kids.

196

Be Firm, but Flexible

Often, people working flexible schedules allow themselves to creep back into their old schedule. For example, you might hold your Monday, Wednesday, and Friday schedule consistently for a few months. But then someone schedules a meeting you should attend on a Tuesday, so you come in. The meeting becomes a weekly meeting so you start coming in every Tuesday, and you check your e-mail while there. Coworkers notice your availability on Tuesdays and stop to ask you questions. Before you know it, your schedule has become Monday, Tuesday, Wednesday, and Friday.

You can avoid this by staying firm in your availability. If you say you won't check messages when out of the office, don't check messages. If someone asks you to attend a meeting on your day off, tell him or her that you cannot attend. Ask if someone else can attend in your place, or if you can just get the minutes from the meeting. If a meeting you need to attend ends up falling on a day off, consider readjusting your schedule and taking a different day off instead of coming in an extra day.

However, you also don't want to become entirely inflexible. Jennifer, who worked part-time as a Human Resource manager at an insurance company, told me she made it a priority to shift her hours when necessary to make it to important meetings and events. Many people worked flexible schedules in her office, and if everyone held too firm to their schedule, it could take weeks or months to get a meeting organized.

Therefore you must be firm, but still flexible. Do not get into the habit of working extra hours or working on your days off. But do so occasionally if it helps support your company's business. Make sure on those occasions that you do need to stay later or come in on an off day that you don't complain about it. When you do need to come in on an off day, consider leaving early another day.

■ ■

When staying firm, don't be afraid to just say, "I have a conflict" if someone wants to meet with you at a time when you have an event with your children. You do not need to justify your need to attend a soccer game instead of a monthly budget meeting if the meeting was scheduled at the last minute.

If you find yourself working more than you agreed to, or if you find that the days you've chosen to have off or work at home days conflict with company needs, consider asking for a change in your schedule. You should try to make this kind of change during the trial period of your arrangement. You should also get feedback from your boss before making a request to change your schedule, as he or she may offer another alternative to help you manage better.

If changing your schedule won't solve the problem of working more hours than you agreed to work, you definitely need to take action. First, you can reevaluate the situation to see what you need to do to cover the work that exceeds your availability. This might include finding someone else to delegate work to, or eliminating some of your responsibilities such as unnecessary reports. If you can't reduce your workload, you may need to renegotiate your salary.

Communicate

You must communicate effectively with your boss and others in order to maintain firm flexibility. You can start by setting expectations with your boss, clients, and coworkers. You should let them know when and how to contact you when you work from home, or if you work reduced or alternate hours. For example Kristin, who works as a part-time IT manager, let her employees and clients know to contact her via e-mail on her off days. She usually responds within a few hours of any e-mail, and if her plans take her away from her computer on a regular day off, she notifies her staff in advance.

You must also communicate with your boss about your work arrangement. Ask your boss for feedback on the arrangement. Is he or she satisfied with your performance? What could you do differently? Better? By soliciting feedback from your boss, you can make sure you address any concerns before they become problems.

Take Control of Your Time

Working parents must have strong time-management skills. You must take control of your time so you do not waste the precious time you have doing mundane things or working more than you need to when you could be spending time with your children.

To take control of your time, I suggest a four-step process. Start by getting organized. We all waste a lot of time looking for things or sorting through our stuff to get to the work we need done. Even if you face a disaster in your house or office, a few days spent cleaning it up will pay off.

Invest in some organizers for you house and your workspace. Think about things you use on a daily basis and things you use rarely. Those that you use rarely should be stored away. Those things you use often should be within easy reach. You also want to make sure your keep your work files well-organized. If you need to direct someone to find a file for you in your office while working from home, you want to make sure your helper can easily find things. Consider hiring a professional organizer to help get you organized.

Four Steps to Taking Control of Your Time

1. Get organized.
2. Commit to a planning system.
3. Elimitate time-wasters.
4. Overcome obstacles.

You must next commit to some kind of planning system to keep your calendar and a to-do list. You can use everything from an electronic planner to a yellow note pad. Every day take a look at what you need to get done and write it down. You will feel a great sense of accomplishment by crossing things off your list.

Third, eliminate the time-wasters in your life. Do you spend hours each evening surfing the Internet? While you should stay in touch with others and stay up-to-date on the world around you, try scheduling some specific time for Internet activity and limit yourself each day. Wouldn't you rather spend that time with your children? At home you can also find a lot of extra time if you limit the amount of TV you watch each night. If you put the kids to bed and then watch TV for even just two hours each night, you end up spending the equivalent of one full month each year just watching TV!

You can also take many small steps to get more time in your day. For example, I try to only buy clothing that does not need ironing. Sound silly to you? Well, I bent my rule and bought a blouse last week that requires ironing. I blew 20 minutes of my evening getting it in shape to wear tomorrow. If I did that every night of the week, I would spend almost five full days a year just ironing instead of spending that time getting paid work done, or better yet, with my children. Would you spend a week away from your children to iron clothes?

You can also avoid time-wasters at work. Save socializing for the lunch hour, and try to get out of unnecessary meetings. If you work from home, or have to go out and see clients, make sure you always confirm meetings. I have wasted a lot of time showing up for meetings that don't happen.

Finally, you must overcome personal obstacles when trying to manage your time. Perfectionism causes the most problems for working parents, particularly mothers. To have a truly family-friendly work life, you must give up your dream of becoming perfect in every way. Remember why your company and your family value you. You didn't become the top-selling sales representative at your office because you have a neat desk. Your kids don't love you because you have up-to-date scrapbooks. Focus your time on the things that matter. If you can't give it up altogether, try being just a little less perfect in one area. For example, as I mentioned earlier, I have let my housekeeping skills lapse.

Many of us also procrastinate, which causes you to waste time trying to avoid doing something. First of all, if you keep a to-do list, force yourself to keep to it. Also, don't wait for a block of time to work on a project. Do small pieces. Recently, I wanted to get some of my pictures into a photo album. I kept waiting for a free weekend to work on it, but of course that never came, so I broke it down. One day I sorted the pictures. The next day I started putting them in the album. A few weeks later I found an hour to sit down and label them. Finally, reward yourself for getting things done! Whether a bowl of your favorite ice cream, or a massage at the local spa, a reward goes a long way in motivating you to do the things you don't want to do.

Working Together

Whether both partners in a relationship works in an alternate arrangement, you must pull together as a team to approach raising your family. If one spouse works a part-time schedule, you must spell out how to manage home responsibilities. One friend confided in me that she feared if she went part-time, her husband would expect her to take over all of the housework on her day off. While you should expect the spouse working less to take on more of the housework, the full-time working parent needs to take on some responsibility as well. If you cut back your hours at work, you probably did so to become more involved with your children, not so you can do more housework.

Working with some flexibility takes a lot of juggling. You need to make an effort to stay on the same page. This morning my husband and I spent a half of an hour just going through our calendar making sure we have all of our needs covered. He marks in his calendar evenings that he must be home on time or even early. He also notes days in which I have no flexibility, such as when I have a speaking engagement. He tries to keep those days open from commitments that would be difficult to get out of, such as a meeting with a new client. I make notes in my calendar of evenings when he must entertain clients or when he will be out of town. By knowing the others' availability to cover in a pinch, we can better avoid last-minute emergencies.

Involve Your Kids

The more your children understand what you do, the more they will learn to support you. Involve your kids in your work as much as possible, so they understand what you do when not with them. Through involving your kids in your work, you can help mesh your worlds together better.

I sometimes grade papers while my kids color or work on a craft activity. We say that we are all working. My kids have also visited my classroom and met some of my students. They tell their friends about "mommy's school." My friend Jill, who invests in real estate, often must spend time remodeling or updating homes she has purchased. When possible, she involves the kids, letting them help her paint or drawing on drywall before she installs it.

When Amy found that her work schedule would not work with her daughter's kindergarten schedule, she took up her boss's offer and brought her daughter to work. Amy works in a local decorating store, and her 5-year-old daughter not only accompanies her to the store for a few hours each Tuesday before she catches the bus, but she also actually gets involved in Mom's work. She charms the store's customers while handing out paint stir sticks and pressing the right button to print out their receipts.

If you work outside of home, bring examples of your work home so your kids know what you do. An advertising executive can show off the ads she designed. An attorney can tell stories about working in a courtroom. The kids might act as though they don't care about your work, but I have heard from many teachers how children proudly tell their classmates about their parents' work.

You must also teach your children about finances and how money works from an early age. The more your children understand that work provides food, someplace to live, and the toys or activities they enjoy, the more understanding they will have about your need to work as they grow older. Especially if you work part-time, or have pursued a less lucrative career path in order to spend more time with your children. If they know such a decision impacts the choice between a new bike and spending time with you, they will likely understand why they can't have a new bike. Well, maybe they won't understand at 4 years old, but as they grow into adults, they will appreciate your choice.

Chapter Wrap-Up

Getting a family-friendly work arrangement in place is only the first step in creating a life that allows you to balance your work and home. You must also work hard to keep the arrangement satisfactory to you and your company. Very rarely does everything go perfectly from day one. Understanding this will help ease your frustration as things go wrong. Know that things will go wrong; when they do, closely examine the problem, and find a solution that will not compromise your priorities.

Resources

Websites

National Association of Professional Organizers: *www.napo.net*

Books

151 Quick Ideas to Manage Your Time and Organize Your Life by Robert E. Dittmer (Career Press, 2006).

How to Say No Without Feeling Guilty: And Say Yes to More Time, and What Matters Most to You by Patti Breitman and Connie Hatch (Broadway Books, 2001).

Leave the Office Earlier by Laura Stack (Broadway Books, 2004).

Chapter

18

Managing a Family-Friendly Career

I wish I could promise you that a family-friendly work arrangement will not affect your career. For many, it will not. My flexible work has actually created more opportunities for me. For example, if I stayed in a traditional work arrangement, I wouldn't have had the opportunity to write this book. However, an alternate work arrangement, particularly a reduced-hour schedule, can impact your career. Stepping away from a traditional career path will often take you out of the running for the next promotion. Fortunately, you can take some steps to ensure that you successfully move forward in your career, regardless of your schedule.

Many parents successfully manage a family-friendly career. That is, they forge an alternate work arrangement and still proceed to climb the ladder at their company. For example, LuAnne requested one of the first part-time positions at her consulting company more than 15 years ago following the birth of her first child. This was a bold move in a corporate culture where success meant that you put in the hours and traveled frequently. As her children are now teenagers, she still keeps a part-time schedule while continuing to progress in her career.

Continuing to progress in your career will create some specific challenges. Some parents choose to take an alternate work schedule for just a short period of time and put their career progress on hold. However, you have other options. You can

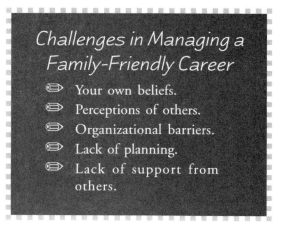

Challenges in Managing a Family-Friendly Career

➥ Your own beliefs.

➥ Perceptions of others.

➥ Organizational barriers.

➥ Lack of planning.

➥ Lack of support from others.

still pursue a rewarding and growing career while working in a family-friendly arrangement. It just may take some additional intentional efforts. The following sections outline some of the challenges you will face, and provide direction in overcoming these challenges.

Your Own Beliefs

Often, parents working in an alternate work arrangement become their own worst enemy. If you believe that your work arrangement will limit your career opportunities, then it probably will. You may decide that you do not want to move up the career ladder during a certain period in your life. When your children need a lot of your time and attention, you may choose to "lay low" and just maintain the status quo for a few years. You can continue to have a rewarding work life without jumping on the next rung of the career ladder.

However, don't just assume that because you work in an alternate arrangement, you can't move ahead in your organization. If those working alternate schedules continue to consistently put their careers on hold, alternate work arrangements will never become the norm. If you want to continue progressing in your career, find out your next step and start working on what you need to do to get promoted. Start figuring out if and how you can apply your current work arrangement in the next level of the organization. Start marketing your success around your organization so that others can see that such an arrangement can work. You must think about your future now, and take some action to keep your career going. Moving ahead in any company requires some business savvy, but even more so when working in an alternate arrangement.

I have a quote posted by my desk: "If you can imagine it, you can achieve it." Your mindset helps determine your success in an alternate work arrangement. You must exude confidence. If others see that you don't think your arrangement will hurt you then they may begin believing it themselves.

The Perception Problem

And here lies your greatest challenge. The perception your coworkers have of your work arrangement creates one of the biggest dilemmas faced by those working alternate schedules. If you have found a truly family-friendly culture where lots of people work alternate schedules, then you may not have a problem. But if you are the first, or one of only a few that have taken advantage of a company's willingness to accommodate family needs, then you may face some questioning looks when you get ready to leave for the day at 3 p.m. on Friday.

While you know that you will not rush home to catch your favorite TV show, and will likely be checking e-mail later in the evening, others may not believe you. You really only need to ignore the stares, and proceed with your work proudly. Remember that you chose this arrangement; do not let others judge you for the decision you have made for your family. However, it may be worth your time to take some actions to change other's perceptions of your arrangement.

First, set out your new arrangement at the beginning. Co-workers will more likely gossip and speculate if they do not know the details. Tell them about your arrangement. If necessary and relevant, remind them also that your cut in hours results in a cut in pay.

If you still feel the stares or suspect that you have become the object of office gossip, you can also confront the situation head on. At a staff meeting, or just in the lunchroom, tell your coworkers that you sense they disapprove of your work arrangement. Ask them why. Then, explain that you worked hard to develop a proposal, and you made the business case for your arrangement. Offer to coach others who would prefer a similar arrangement. Most often, the disapproval of others comes out of envy.

Further, take steps to demonstrate that you still get your work done. If you work late into the evening, drop the staff an e-mail to make sure they know how late you might work at home. This may seem like a silly and trivial thing to do, and if you feel above it, then by all means don't compromise your beliefs. But gentle reminders to others that you may be working after they have called it a day go a long way in reminding others of your work habits.

It is okay to conceal that you work part-time

Many of my clients don't know that I officially only work part-time. Part of me wants to make a big announcement to everyone that I do work part-time because I shouldn't be ashamed of that fact. I should be proud that I have managed a work situation that allows me to spend time with my family.

However, I still often conceal my arrangement. Because I service clients, I don't want them to take their business elsewhere because they have concerns about my availability. I know that I can make special arrangements in the event of an urgent work need. But I also know that few things in my line of work can't wait until tomorrow. Further, sometimes I think it makes a good impression to be a little unavailable. I am in demand! They don't need to know that on some days, I am in demand only with the toddler crowd.

Organizational Barriers

If you've landed at a family-friendly company, you should avoid many organizational barriers. However, if you are among the first to create an alternate work arrangement at a company, you may face some significant challenges in your career progression. Often, organizational policies and practices will be what limits your ability to move forward in your career.

As discussed in Chapter 6, a company's culture can make an alternate work arrangement challenging. If you work in a culture where an alternate work arrangement lies outside of the norm, moving forward in your career may take some extra work. Often, when only a few work alternate work arrangements at a company, many assume that those working an alternate schedule want to only focus on their family and not their career. To combat this challenge, talk often of your desire to move forward in your company. In regular meetings with your boss, ask about ways to prepare yourself for your next promotion. When given the opportunity to meet with higher-level managers, make sure you talk clearly about your future with the company.

Stay connected. If you work in an alternate arrangement, particularly if from home, you can get out of the loop and lose touch with your coworkers. Make extra efforts to make it to important meetings. Use e-mail to keep in touch.

You can also benefit through finding a mentor in your organization. Someone at a higher level in your organization can help you maneuver the political path to overcome barriers to moving forward. Ideally, another working parent can walk you through many of the challenges you face.

Your biggest organizational barrier may be antiquated policies or long-accepted practices that limit opportunities of those that work alternate schedules, particularly part-time schedules. To merit exceptions to the policy, you must provide support for your position. Therefore, you must make extra efforts to make sure your boss and other leaders in the organization understand your value to the company, despite your alternate schedule. A few tips:

✏ Make sure your boss knows how hard you work. Toot your own horn. When you get a complimentary e-mail from a client, forward it to your boss. Respond as quickly as possible if your boss leaves you a message. Avoid the old adage "out of sight, out of mind."

✏ Make your family a priority, but don't neglect your job. For example, if you need to take the afternoon off to attend an event at your child's school, make an extra effort to get the report due first thing in the morning completed before you leave. Employers value highly conscientious employees. Your company will appreciate your ability to get your job done, even while working an alternate schedule.

✏ Look for opportunities to be flexible for your company. Let your coworkers know they can count on you when in a bind. While you need to stick to your schedule and not be taken advantage of, being completely rigid will only make you seem difficult.

✏ Track your performance. If you need to leave your company or move to another position, you will benefit from having documented evidence of your success in an alternate work arrangement. Keep copies of your performance reviews or other reports of your abilities and accomplishments.

Lack of Planning

If you have an arrangement that works for you now, don't get too comfortable. Your needs will change some time in the future, and you must now start putting your plan and resources in place to prepare yourself for that change. Your children will grow and their needs will change. Your work opportunities may change. Right now I have a great arrangement; but eventually I know I want to teach college full-time. At that point, I won't have the same flexibility. However, I will most likely have kids in school by then, so my schedule will have more stability. Basically, I have already started thinking now about the family-friendly work I need in a few years.

Consider how your family needs will change as your children grow. Many parents find that, as their children become teenagers, they want to be around the house more. They may choose to cut back their hours, or just work from home to keep an eye on things. At some point, you may determine that you want to stay at home for a period of time. If so, read Chapter 20 and make sure you make efforts to keep yourself marketable while at home. The more you can think ahead about your needs, the more you can prepare and position yourself to create a family-friendly arrangement.

Lack of Support From Others

Trying to negotiate the path to a family-friendly work arrangement on your own will cause frustration, as well as missed opportunities. You must ask for support from others. As parents, you will need to continue to communicate your priorities, plans, and needs with each other. If you find your arrangement is not working as you expected, talk about it before it becomes stressful for you. Talk to your boss or your spouse. Talk to your friends to get advice. Just remember, you are not in this alone. Even a single parent with few resources can find many others out there facing the same challenges. Reach out to them for help.

If you have successfully structured your own alternate work schedule and achieved success in your career, help others achieve the same success that you have found. You can become a resource in your own company by sharing your alternate work proposal so others can get an idea on how to structure a proposal. Start a support group for parents at your organization. You could work to identify, research, and recommend family-friendly programs and benefits.

If you'd like to connect with other parents outside of your company, numerous online discussion boards for both men and women allow you to participate in online discussions and give advice to others. From MySpace to Yahoo groups, you can find working parent groups easily. Through sharing your experience, you can possibly help others one at a time. Further, these boards may help you at some point. Often, others share their ideas, tips, and tricks for making it work.

If you do find time to volunteer or support other organizations, look to support those that help parents better manage work and family. Write to your legislators to support legislation that helps families manage. Only through individual efforts will we live in a world that does not need a book such as this to find work that works with family.

Chapter Wrap-Up

A family-friendly work arrangement requires planning and constant effort. If you have a work arrangement that works, you must make efforts to ensure you can keep it. Further, you must also be constantly looking ahead to determine your next move. You can fashion a family-friendly career by forging ahead from one alternate arrangement to the next. The look of your career can change over time. At some periods, you may be moving ahead full force, while at others, you may be at a complete standstill. The key is to have a plan, and make sure you keep it in sync with your family.

Resources

Online Networking

Club Mom: *www.clubmom.com*

A mom-to-mom social networking site. Includes discussion boards for working moms.

Mommy Track'd: *www.mommytrackd.com*

It is a multi-tasking site that offers busy working moms a resource to help manage the daily tug of war between work and family. Includes a discussion forum to allow you to meet other working moms.

Help Others

9to5, National Association of Working Women: *www.9to5.org*

A national, grassroots membership organization that strengthens women's ability to work for economic justice.

Families and Work Institute: *www.familiesandwork.org*
A nonprofit center for research that provides data to inform decision-making on the changing workforce, changing family and changing community.

Labor Project for Working Families: *www.laborproject.org*
A national, nonprofit advocacy and policy organization providing technical assistance, resources, and education to unions and union members on family issues in the workplace.

National Partnership for Women and Families: *www.nationalpartnership.org*
A nonprofit, nonpartisan organization that uses public education and advocacy to promote fairness in the workplace, quality healthcare, and policies that help women and men meet the dual demands of work and family.

Parents without Partners: *www.parentswithoutpartners.org*
National organization that provides support to single parents in the way of discussions, professional speakers, study groups, publications and social activities for families and adults.

Women Work!: *www.womenwork.org*
The National Network for Women's Employment is a nonprofit, nonpartisan organization that advances economic justice and equality for women through education, advocacy, and organizing.

Chapter

19

Going It Alone

Many parents create their own family-friendly work. Some take this path because they have a true entrepreneurial spirit. Others need income and don't see any other way to work it out. However, many parents don't consider the option of working on their own because they find the idea of starting a business intimidating and overwhelming. Before you put aside the idea of going it alone, remember you do not need to necessarily open up a retail store or rent office space to start a business. You also don't have to make it a full-time venture.

Many parents going it alone take a more simple approach. For example, you could start your own business by selling items you find at garage sales on eBay. You start a business venture any time you pursue work that generates income. Such a pursuit should be taken with some consideration. And with a little work, any self-employment option can be a rewarding way to make money and also fulfill your professional aspirations.

Working for Yourself

No one cares for your needs more than you do. So, why not be the boss? Why answer to someone else if you can make it on your own? By working on your own, you can best guarantee the schedule you want. As the boss, you set your schedule and you decide how much to work.

If you want a flexible work option, then you should pursue a business opportunity that meets that need. For example, you may enjoy cooking, but starting a restaurant will require you to work long hours away from your family for lunch and dinner (and possibly breakfast, too). While no list of right or wrong business opportunities exist, certain characteristics of some options provide more flexibility.

For example, Jill quit her full-time office job, but missed the challenge her work provided. She decided to start investing in real estate. After taking some classes (back to Chapter 4), she purchased her first investment home. After a few weeks of work she resold the property with a significant profit and her business was launched. She found quickly that this work provided her the flexibility she needed. She could check out new properties or work on a remodel any time she wanted. Further, she did this with her kids in tow. The kids go with her to check out houses, and she also completes much of the handy work with her kids along. They help her work or entertain themselves with activities she brings along.

Who succeeds?

While working on your own provides many advantages, it also creates more personal challenges than working for someone else. While experts exist to help you out, you must figure out how to proceed on a daily basis. Successful solo workers must:

- Be self-motivated and disciplined. If you only work hard when your boss has an eye on you, then working on your own may not be a good option.

- Be resourceful and creative. You will often need to solve a problem on your own, or creatively find time in your limited to schedule to accomplish work. Without a creative inclination, this will create a challenge.

- Be willing to accept failures, because you will likely face them. You must be able to learn from mistakes and keep your confidence as you bounce back from an obstacle.

Family-Friendly Business Ideas

Many business options offer flexibility, particularly those that you can start from home. A business from home offers many advantages for a working parent. You face less up-front investment because you do not have to secure office or storefront space. You can also work more flexible hours if you don't have to deal with a commute.

Family-Friendly Business Ideas

- Consulting.
- Independent sales.
- Web-based business.
- Franchising.
- Childcare.
- Creating something to sell.
- Providing a service.
- Mystery shopping.

However, you can also create a business away from your home that offers you the flexibility you need. Endless options exist for either alternative. I've listed several books with business advice at the conclusion of this chapter. The following list identifies some business opportunities that may offer certain advantages to a working parent.

Consulting

If you currently work in a professional field, you most easily can move out on your own by starting a consulting business. After several years working in corporate Human Resources departments, I found I could easily market my expertise to smaller companies. Independent consultants work in marketing, accounting, public relations, training, engineering, and many other fields. Consider partnering with other professional service providers to start building a client base. I partner with my husband's accounting firm and get most of my clients without having to do a lot of marketing of my services.

Independent sales consultant

Opportunities abound for independent sales consultants. As an independent sales consultant, you sell another company's products through several channels. Through home parties, catalog, and Website sales, you can generate income with a lot of flexibility. This type of venture usually involves some investment. Most companies require that you purchase sample products to use in your in-home demonstrations. From there, you can sell as much or as little as you choose. Some Websites at the end of this chapter provide guidance in selecting a company to represent.

Most independent sales representatives find success when they represent a product that they truly believe in, so consider something you like. However, be careful to check and make sure that the product has not already been oversold in your geographic area. That is, check and see how many other sales consultants live in your area before proceeding. You will have challenges finding new sales leads if many people already sell the product in your area.

You can also expand your services beyond just selling a product. For example, if you represent a scrapbook supply company, consider offering a service to assemble scrapbooks for busy moms. You can profit from the scrapbook supplies as well as get paid for your service. Or if you sell home decorating items, consider offering a decorating service to help others redecorate their homes.

Web-based business

A Web-based business provides many opportunities to work with flexibility. You of course first need a business idea. But with the help of a Website designer, you can fairly easily get a site up and running with only a small investment. Numerous business options exist. You can provide a service such as resume writing or typing, or you can sell products. Web-based businesses, however, must attract enough traffic to the site to actually make money. Before you start a Web-based business, you must consider how you will attract enough customers to make a profit.

You don't have to develop your own Website to make money selling online. Many parents have made some profits through selling items online. A variety of methods exist to obtain products that you can then sell online on Website such as eBay or Amazon. Tammy tells me that she sells items on eBay often. For example, she recently snapped up several dress-up outfits for a few dollars each when a popular character store closed at the mall, and resold them on eBay for 10 times that amount, yielding a significant profit for little work effort.

Franchising

Purchasing a franchise means you purchase the right to use a business concept, logos, service protocols, and so on. The franchise business also usually provides you with training and other resources to get your business started and make it a success. Many different types of franchises exist, including fast-food restaurants, fitness centers, and even some home-based business targeting parents such as Stroller Moms, a workout program for moms with strollers. The company trains the franchise owner on how to run a class, and the class can meet at a local park or perhaps a community center.

A franchise can be an expensive start-up option, but it comes with many of the resources and much of the expertise that you need. Essentially, you get all of the support that you need to start a business. However, you must make the effort to write a business plan and determine if a particular franchise offers a viable profit opportunity for your particular geographic area. You should also work with an accountant or some other professional to evaluate a franchise opportunity.

Childcare

If you want to stay at home with your kids but need income, you may want to consider opening a home-based childcare. If you choose this option, you should first check with your state to ensure you comply with regulations on home-based childcare centers.

A childcare business succeeds if you treat it as a business. The first childcare provider I worked with actually asked me to sign a contract when I started bringing my son to her. I appreciated the contract because it clearly spelled out how things would work. The contract specified the childcare fees, due dates, and late penalties. It spelled out what kind of illness required me to keep my sick child at home. The contract also outlined paid holiday and vacation time, which she deserved, but I honestly wouldn't have thought of providing. I referred to the contract many times and appreciated her effort to ensure that we had a business relationship. Too often, home childcare providers get taken advantage of and a contract can help avoid the problem.

Do research in your area to find out the going rate for childcare. Be sure to account for the cost of food and other supplies. Parents must typically provide diapers and baby food, but this should be spelled out in advance. States often offer resources to home-based childcare providers. This might include funding for nutritious meals or equipment, such as portable cribs or safety gates.

Create something to sell

Many parents create something for their kids that they later determine they can sell to other parents. Sometimes referred to as "parentprenuers," these start-up businesses often work well with family life. Julie Aigner-Clark, the founder of Baby Einstein originally made videos for her daughter. Other parents showed interest, and years later she is a millionaire after selling her company to The Walt Disney Company. Do you do anything special or creative for your children that others would benefit from?

If you have some talent or creative capabilities, you might be able to generate some income making and selling crafts. Creating crafts provides a very flexible work pursuit; you can shop and make your craft on your own schedule. You may even be able to involve your kids in your projects. Crafts can be sold in many different ways. You can sell at community fairs or fundraisers, or you can sell your crafts online, or at local and regional craft fairs as well.

If you have a green thumb, you may grow fruits and vegetables to sell out of your front yard, or at a community market. Handmade gifts such as candles, soap, or jewelry can be sold at local shops or through a Website or catalog. Anything you can create and sell holds a potential business opportunity.

Providing a service

Other busy parents need help managing their home or personal business. Endless options exist to provide a service to others.

For example, you could run errands, go grocery shopping, wash cars, or many other things. You may already do many of these things for your family. Often called concierge services, this kind of business provides a perfect work opportunity for parents.

I talked to a woman last year who ran garage sales for others. She would go in and help people clean out their house and identify items. She then would clean and price them, and set up the garage sale. She would handle advertising, post signs, and sometimes work the sale. Many other parents similar to you need help managing often-overwhelming responsibilities. Such needs create many business opportunities.

Mystery shopping and focus groups

If you like to shop, you should enjoy the opportunity to get paid for shopping. Many organizations hire mystery or secret shoppers to pose as a customer and then submit a report on the company. Usually the client company, often a restaurant or a retail store, hires a mystery shopping company to coordinate the mystery shopping. You sign up for assignments on a Website and usually have to submit your report via the Website as well.

You will not get rich mystery shopping. You will get free lunches here and there and be able to pick up free products and sometime a small amount of cash. You can also build your resume. If you stay-at-home, you can note that you worked as a mystery shopper (or better yet a "customer service evaluator"), and that this built many skills such as observation to detail, learning about quality and customer service, and submitting detailed reports.

Never pay for the opportunity to mystery shop. Hundreds of legitimate companies exist that provide mystery shopping services, and they do not charge you a fee to register. Also, keep in mind that sometimes the mystery shopping client requests that you do not bring children with you on a shop. Toni, who supplements her income through mystery shopping enjoys it because she gets paid for doing things she already needs to do, such as going to the grocery store. She enjoys the extra money, but cautions that you really can't rely on making enough to pay the bills. How much work you can find depends on the availability of shops in your area and how many other shoppers you compete against for the shops.

You can also make a little extra money by participating in focus groups. Again, it does not provide a reliable income, but it does provide an interesting and sometimes fun experience that can bring you extra cash. Marketing research firms pay people to participate in focus groups for many different types of clients. You may be asked to try a product and provide feedback or even provide your reactions to advertisements. Often, you receive great pay for a short period of time. I've participated in several focus groups earning from $50–$150 for just a few hours of my time. You can identify focus group opportunities by finding marketing research companies in your area.

Working Together

Some couples take the leap together. You may not have the skills and the time to start a business on your own, but possibly with your partner's help you can get a company up and running. The financial risk creates the biggest challenge. Many people start businesses with the safety net of their spouse's income, which doesn't exist if you both pursue a new business opportunity full-time. You must also determine if working together works for your relationship.

Success on Your Own

You must take your business venture seriously. While this chapter provides some general guidance, you must make an effort to learn more about how to run a business. Check out what kind of local start-up support you can access. Many cities and geographic areas have economic development initiatives that help new businesses get off the ground. These opportunities often have extra benefits for businesses run by women or minorities to increase the diversity of business ownership within the community. If necessary, involve the right professionals to help you get your business started. For example, an investment in an accountant or lawyer to help you get your business established will likely save you money and headaches later.

Keeping your business family-friendly

Consider the scope of what you want to do. You do not need to necessarily start a full-fledged business taking hundreds of hours each week. Often, people intending to spend more time with their family by working for themselves end up spending less time because they spend so much time getting the business up and running.

If you want to create a more family-friendly work environment, make sure you manage your workload appropriately. Often, when starting a business, you may feel you need to accept any work offers you receive. I do this in my own consulting work. Worried that I might not have more work coming, I take on a new client when I don't really have time. When this happens, my work becomes overwhelming and I have to take more time away from my children. Also, do not create unrealistic deadlines in order to satisfy customers if it will stretch you too thin. Remember to factor in your family obligations when estimating how long a project will take you to complete.

Watch out for work-at-home scams

Be careful; a lot of scams target stay-at-home parents that want to make money through flexible work. Some home-based businesses require an investment, such as a franchise purchase fee or the need for independent sellers to purchase their own samples. But you should carefully evaluate any spending requirements for a business opportunity. Make sure you know exactly what you get for the fee and that the fee is reasonable.

Be cautious of any Website or opportunity that doesn't exactly tell you what kind of work you will do. If you have to sign-up and provide personal information (or worse yet, a credit card) before they give you details about the opportunity, then I would caution to stay away. Carefully check out any business option you choose to pursue. Resources such as the Better Business Bureau and the Federal Trade Commission can provide you valuable insight on varying business opportunities.

Chapter Wrap-Up

If you decide to go it alone, you have many options. In fact, you can take up more than one option. I do consulting work on the side to supplement my income while teaching part-time. My child's current sitter also has a part-time sales job that has very flexible work requirements. My friend Sandi does sewing alterations and also works contract editing assignments.

If you choose to do your own thing, whether making crafts to sell or starting your own restaurant, take pride in what you do. I can't tell you how parents tell me that they don't work, they "just sell stuff on eBay," or they "just watch kids." If you generate income for work you do, then you should consider yourself "employed." Embrace it!

Resources

Books on Going It Alone

101 Best Home-Based Businesses for Women, 3rd Edition: Everything You Need to Know About Getting Started on the Road to Success (For Fun & Profit) by Priscilla Huff (Three Rivers Press, 2002).

401 Questions Every Entrepreneur Should Ask by James L. Silvester (Career Press, 2006).

Capitalizing on Being Woman Owned by Janet W. Christy (Career Press, 2006).

Full-Time Woman, Part-Time Career by Karen Steede-Terry (CMS Press, 2005).

How to Buy, Sell, and Profit on eBay: Kick-Start Your Home-Based Business in Just Thirty Days by Adam Ginsberg (Collins, 2005).

The Mom Inventors Handbook: How to Turn Your Great Idea into the Next Big Thing by Tamara Monosoff (McGraw Hill, 2005).

Business Start-Up Resources

Better Business Bureau: *www.bbb.org*
You can search for business names and find out if the company has any consumer complaints.

The Entreprenuerial Parent: *www.en-parent.com*
A resource for parents starting their own business, includes professional career counseling, quick-tip articles, and inspirational profiles.

Federal Trade Commission: *www.ftc.gov/ftc/consumer.htm*
You can research complaints on business opportunities. Check out the "Franchise and Business Opportunities" link.

International Franchise Association: *www.franchise.org*
Provides basic guidance plus links to franchise opportunities.

National Business Incubator Association: *www.nbia.org*
Has a directory you can search to find a business incubator in your area.

NE Mothers: *http://nemothers.blogspot.com*
Reports work-at-home scams.

SCORE: *www.score.org*
Non-profit providing free advice to entrepreneurs.

Small Business Administration: Small Business Development Center: *www.sba.gov/sbdc*
Government resource that provides guidance and resources to small business owners.

Small Office Home Office: *www.soho.org*
Provides support to people working at home.

Working Today: *www.workingtoday.org*
Nonprofit that supports independent workers. Offers opportunity to buy health insurance.

Mystery Shopping and Direct Sales

About.com Mystery Shopper Guide: *http://jobsearch.about.com/od/mysteryshopper*
Explains mystery shopping and provides directory of companies.

Open Directory Project: *http://dmoz.org/Business/Customer_Service/Mystery_Shopping*
Nonprofit organization provides a directory of mystery shopping.

Direct Selling Opportunities: *www.directsellingopportunities.com*
Comprehensive resources for independent sales business. Includes directory of direct sales companies.

Business Resources for Women

Direct Selling Women's Alliance: *www.dswa.org*
A professional association for women who sell products through home parties or networking. Articles provide guidance in selecting a business opportunity and creating success with your venture.

Home Based Working Moms: *www.hbwm.com*
A networking group for moms working at home.

Ladies Who Launch: *www.ladieswholaunch.com*
A fully integrated online and offline worldwide network and information source that provides the tools and resources to women launching businesses and creative projects.

National Association of Women Business Owners: *www.nawbo.org*
Networking and support group for women business owners.

Work At Home Mom: *www.wahm.com*
An online magazine with useful ideas for moms working from home.

Moms-for-Profit: *www.momsforprofit.com*
A business development agency specializing in mom-owned businesses. All services are provided by their talent pool of professional women turned stay-at-home mom consultants.

The Mom Pack: *www.mompack.com*
A group of moms in business who work together in an innovative free advertising partnership. Membership is free and members promote each other's business and also share ideas and advice.

Chapter

20

Staying
Home—
Staying
Marketable

Making the decision to stay at home with your children does not mean you have to abandon all career aspirations. In fact, spending some time at home can give you enough distance from work to allow you to reevaluate your career plans. You may decide to head in a new direction, or continue in the same direction with a newfound focus and passion.

For some, staying home factors into an overall work and family balance plan. The term "sequencing" describes the career plan of a parent who chooses to spend some time at home while planning to return to work at a later time. Some parents sequence throughout their children's upbringing by staying home with infants, returning to work when the kids start school, and then staying at home again later in the challenging teenage years.

I would love to tell you that time out of the workforce does not matter, that you will easily glide back into a work routine with little effort regardless of how long you spend at home. Unfortunately, staying at home often creates obstacles to return to work. A woman at a career-search seminar I gave recently told me that she had just started interviewing after 10 years out of the workforce. She found herself greeted with shocking questions such as, "what exactly have you been doing for 10 years?"

You can possibly minimize these challenges through planning before and while you stay at home. You should consider your possible return even if you may not actually return to work. You must prepare to take care of yourself and your children on your own. Through death, illness, or divorce, you might become the primary breadwinner for your family. Through actively building or maintaining your skills, you can make yourself more marketable to eventually return to work. Most of the things you can do coincide with your responsibilities raising your children, managing your home, and contributing to your community.

Taking On a New Direction

Time at home provides a great opportunity to consider a career change. You can take the time to research and explore different fields. Time away from work gives you some perspective on what you like and don't like about work. Time spent with family can help you figure out your priorities as well as your passions. Further, time at home provides opportunities to build skills to prepare you for a new career.

For example, Amy worked for many years as an information technology (IT) programmer and analyst. But a desire to spend time with her two young daughters, along with a lack of fulfillment in her current job and challenges with her husband's schedule led her to stay home. While her IT career had always been good to her, Amy had talked about changing to a career in interior design for many years. But she never had a chance to pursue it. After a few years at home, she started making the transition to a new career in interior design by working part-time at a local paint and decorating store. Through this opportunity, she has started her path toward a career as a successful designer.

Actively Keeping Sharp

If you plan to continue down the same career path once you return to work, you can take several steps to keep your skills and your job search capability up to date. Further, some of the same activities can build skills to help you transition to a new career path. You should begin pursuing and keeping track of these activities as soon as you make the decision to stay home.

Your network

As I explained in Chapter 12, you must have an active network in the family-friendly job search. You must keep your network active and growing while at home. Keep in touch with your former coworkers as well as others you know in your profession. E-mail makes this task easy. Ask your former boss to keep you on the company e-mail system if possible, so you continue to receive company newsletters and announcements.

You need to also make sure you get some face time with your network. Find a babysitter once a month to have lunch with a network contact. Consider partnering with another stay-at-home parent

Keeping Sharp

- Keep and expand your network.
- Look for opportunities or temporary work.
- Take a class.
- Attend a conference.
- Stay up to date.
- Keep certifications current.
- Volunteer.
- Raising your family.

to watch each other's children while you network. You can also continue to attend professional meetings or other networking opportunities.

Look for ways to expand your network using the guidance provided in Chapter 12. I suggest having simple business cards printed with your name and contact information. You can use these to hand out at parties, the coffee shop, or even at playgroup when you meet a good networking contact.

Special projects

Look for opportunities to work on short-term projects. You can often find these with your former company or through a networking contact. Companies often need people to do short-term projects. Cathy, an engineer turned stay-at-home mom, occasionally works on extra projects for her former employer. She works mostly on these short-term commitments from home. While she typically only works a few days every few months, she can stay up to date in her field. Her former boss also appreciates her willingness to help out. This appreciation will likely be useful when, and if, she returns to work.

You may also find opportunities through friends or family. Jennifer, a former public relations/event-planner turned stay-at-home mom, helps friends organize parties. She also helps her mother-in-law, a business owner, publicize her business through writing press releases and creating marketing materials. These small projects help Jennifer keep her skills sharp and creative abilities active.

You can also look for opportunities to take on temporary assignments through an agency. Often, organizations bring on temporary workers to cover leaves of absences or other short-term needs. For example, you might be able to cover for someone taking a maternity leave. Covering for someone on maternity leave also makes a great contact for a later job share proposition.

Continuing education

Time at home provides a great opportunity to take a class or learn something new in your field, or you may pursue education in a new field. Chip started his own business right out of high school, then married and had children. When his wife recently took on a full-time work opportunity that created a childcare challenge for the couple, Chip took the opportunity to stay-at-home while returning to college to earn a degree.

Chapter 4 covered online education and other family-friendly ways to continue your education or build expertise. More and more college level programs exist that cater to adult students, offering accelerated coursework and flexible schedules. Attending an occasional conference can also help you continue to develop your expertise.

Stay up-to-date in your field

You must stay tuned to changes and trends in your industry or profession while at home. For example, in my field of human resource management, new legislation comes up every few years. Even if I did not continue working regularly, I could easily check in at various government Websites to stay up-to-date. Or just subscribe to a newsletter, professional journal, or some other notification service to find out what's new.

If you plan to return to your previous company, you must to stay up-to-date with company happenings as well. Make sure you receive company newsletters or regularly check the company Website. Your network of former coworkers can also keep you informed.

Keep your certifications current if applicable. Even if you don't know if you will return to work, you should keep these up to date. This might involve attending an occasional workshop or conference, testing, or some other steps. Check in with the certifying organization or board to find out what you need to do to stay active.

Volunteering

I try to limit my volunteer activities as I have a tendency to over commit myself and that challenges any ideas I have about balancing my personal life and family. However, if you stay at home and want to keep your resume active, volunteer activities can be very beneficial.

Look for opportunities to volunteer for activities that relate to your field. For example, if you have just left a career in public relations, volunteer to do publicity for your local PTA group. Seek out nonprofit organizations that might need your help. For example, a former teacher can volunteer as a tutor with an after school program.

If you want to change professions, volunteering can help you gain some valuable experience or develop new skills. Early in my career, I decided to move from sales into human resources. Lacking human resource experience, I volunteered in the human resources department at the American Red Cross. This allowed me to build my expertise and resume enough to get my first job in human resources.

An organization in need of volunteer help will usually accept the offer of someone willing to spend the time, even if they do not have all the right skills and experience. For example, I learned a great deal about marketing as a volunteer for my local animal shelter promoting fundraising events. I did not have any previous marketing experience, but I took on the responsibility when no one else would.

Developing your skills through raising your family

Anyone who has elicited information from a teenager about happenings at school, or negotiated a toy-sharing arrangement with toddlers knows that you develop a lot of skills staying at home that can be valuable in the workplace. I know my Monday morning juggling routine of getting two kids to two different preschools provides an excellent example of my time management skills.

As I discussed in Chapter 14, you should keep a list of stories that provide examples of your experience using particular skills. Make sure you also keep those stories that show the skills you developed at home on that list.

Returning to Work

You have several options to return to work. You may decide to reenter gradually by doing something on your own as discussed in Chapter 19. If you do pursue a traditional job search, Chapter 13 will help you start looking for a family-friendly opportunity. However, time spent at home creates some special challenges in the search process. Through properly preparing your resume and preparing yourself for the interview process, you can overcome the stay-at-home obstacle.

Parenting Skills You Can Use at Work

➥ Negotiation.
➥ Dealing with difficult people.
➥ Motivating and encouraging others.
➥ Time management.
➥ Multi-tasking.
➥ Communication.
➥ Providing leadership.
➥ Integrity.

Source: If You've Raised Kids You Can Manage Anything, by Ann Crittenden, (Gotham Books, 2004).

Updating your resume

Updating your resume to prepare to return to work can be an overwhelming activity. Often, an extremely outdated resume will cause you to practically start over. The solution? Keep your resume up-to-date at all times. Even though I work (and mostly for myself), I still take a look at my resume every month or so to make sure I keep it up to date. Or if I have a new experience or accomplishment to add, I do it right away.

Your volunteer work

You must account for your volunteer work on your resume, looking at in terms of what value it can bring to a future employer. Instead of "Volunteered at animal shelter," try "Increased animal shelter fundraising revenues by 75 percent through creative promotion attracting more than 100 new patrons." Consider the skills you developed through your experience and write your volunteer accomplishments.

Time away from work

You need to account for the gap in your chronological work history while at home; a gap in your resume can mean many things to a recruiter. Did you choose to take time off, or did you get fired and couldn't find another job? While a recruiter will unlikely suspect that you spent time in prison or some other unattractive option, a clear indicator of your time away will help prevent assumptions.

Career experts continue to debate on whether to include your at-home status on your resume. Some believe that if you list your time at home on your resume, a potential employer may pass over you, assuming you don't really want to work. However, I believe you should include your stay-at-home status on your resume. If a company passes on your resume because you indicate that you took some time off to spend with your children, then the company is not family-friendly. Further, including it explains the gap in work history on your resume. Call it what you want, but account for the time.

Chronological or functional resume

If you have been out of the workforce for a long period of time, you may find a functional resume a better approach than a chronological resume. The chronological resume lists your experiences in chronological order, which puts emphasis on your time out of the workforce. The functional resume emphasizes your specific skills or abilities. I believe a functional resume takes the emphasis off of your parenting role, and onto your skills and abilities.

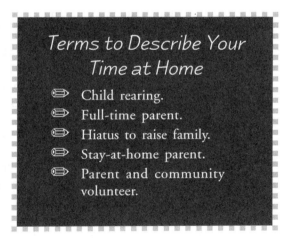

Terms to Describe Your Time at Home

- Child rearing.
- Full-time parent.
- Hiatus to raise family.
- Stay-at-home parent.
- Parent and community volunteer.

Further, a functional resume provides a good format for your resume if you want to transition to a new profession because you can emphasize the transferable skills that you have.

Sample Chronological Resume

Sue S. Smith

100 Main Street Anytown, US 44000

ssmith@service.net (440) 555-1212

OBJECTIVE:

Sales representative opportunity in telecommunications industry.

EXPERIENCE:

Child-rearing, Anytown, US 2001–2006

- Developed strong communication, time management, and multi-tasking skills.
- Chaired Pre-school PTA annual auction fundraiser (2005). Achieved record revenue level through soliciting high price point donations from local vendors.
- Volunteered as Kindergarten registration coordinator (2003–2005). Ensured more than 200 new students received proper registration materials and attended necessary orientation sessions.

BBR Telecommunications, Anytown, US 1997–2001

Senior Account Manager

- Attained $1.8 million in annual sales (FY 2000), exceeding target by $300,000. Ranked as one of the company's top five account managers (out of 20 reps nationwide).
- Increased sales by 15 percent in 1998, 18 percent in 1999, and 20 percent in 2000 by diligently following up on all leads, orchestrating direct mail campaigns, and providing excellent account services.
- Expanded territory sales by contacting all former customers and offering attractive discounts.
- Delivered presentation that led to national contract for networking, computer upgrades, and rentals.

- Negotiated 10-month training contract valued at $250,000.

Mystic Medical Equipment, Anytown, US 1992–1997
Sales Representative

- Marketed and sold medical supplies to an operation with 300 clients. Developed advertising strategies to achieve continued revenue growth. Trained customers in use of medical equipment.
- Often achieved "preferred supplier" status, setting the stage for repeat business with high-profile accounts.
- Facilitated employee meetings, opening lines of communication and promoting acceptance of corporate goal to improve customer relations.
- Established strong vendor relationships, leading to favorable pricing and discounts.

EDUCATION:
Central College, Bachelor of Business Administration, 1992

Sample Functional Resume

Sue S. Smith

100 Main Street Anytown, US 44000

ssmith@service.net (440) 555-1212

OBJECTIVE:
Sales representative opportunity in telecommunications industry.

SUMMARY OF SKILLS:

Marketing and Sales	Project Management
Communication Skills	Customer Service
Computer Skills	Relationship Development
Negotiation	Public Speaking
Events Management	

AREAS OF EFFECTIVENESS:

Marketing/Sales

- Attained $1.8 million in annual sales (FY 2000), exceeding target by $300,000. Ranked as one of the company's top five account managers (out of 20 reps nationwide).
- Consistently increased sales by diligently following up on all leads, orchestrating direct mail campaigns, and providing excellent account services.
- Expanded territory sales by contacting all former customers and offering attractive discounts.
- Often achieved "preferred supplier" status, setting the stage for repeat business with high-profile accounts.
- Achieved record revenue generation through marketing annual PTA auction fundraiser to local businesses leading to donations of high priced auction items.

Organizing/Planning/Communicating

- Expanded sales territory and revenue through developing and executing a plan to systematically target new clients in a specific geographic area.
- Planned sales calls on a weekly basis to optimize exposure of product during business hours.
- Delivered presentation that led to national contract for networking, computer upgrades, and rentals.
- Coordinated Kindergarten registration for more than 200 children. Ensured all students received materials in a timely manner and attended required orientation sessions.

EXPERIENCE:

Child-rearing, Anytown, U.S. 2001–2006

BBR Telecommunications *Senior Account Manager* Anytown, US 1997–2001

Mystic Medical Equipment *Sales Representative* Anytown, U.S.
1992–1997
EDUCATION:
Central College
Bachelor of Business Administration, 1992

Preparing for the Interview

Don't downplay your time at home. You have worked hard raising your children and you should be proud of your accomplishments. Speak proudly of the things you have done with and for your children and your home. As you prepare for the interview as outlined in Chapter 14, make sure you consider your at-home activities when creating your list of stories that illustrate your abilities. Also, talk about what you have done for your community. Even if you haven't done a lot of volunteering, you likely have helped other parents and families. Make sure you have your relevant stories ready to go.

Answering "the question"

Many potential employers will ask you why you chose to stay home. You should consider how you want to answer this question at the same time you make the decision to stay home. The truth is the best response, and if you can outline your decision-making process at the time that you make the decision, you will not need to fabricate an answer. However, while I advocate truthfulness, I caution brutal honesty. For example "I hated my boss and resented her for taking me away from my precious newborn, so I took the opportunity to walk," might hinder your chance to find a job. Further, you should avoid responses to this question that might cause a hiring manager to question your abilities. Telling an interviewer that you quit working because you couldn't manage working and taking care of your child might make the interviewer question your ability to manage both now.

Focus on the fact that you determined this difficult decision was best for you and your family. For example, you might say " I was fortunate to have a financial situation that allowed me to step back and focus on my family," or, " After much deliberation and weighing my alternatives, I decided that I would take the opportunity to spend time my children."

Your response to this question should be clear, logical, and true. You can also take the opportunity when responding to this question to discuss what steps you took during your time at home to prepare for your return to work.

Chapter Wrap-Up

If you plan to stay-at-home whether by choice or because you can't find a work arrangement that works, start thinking now about returning to work. Even if you don't know when or if you will return, you can spend time now preparing. In addition to putting you in a better situation once you want to return, it will also give you something personally fulfilling to focus on in addition to your children.

A little time spent here and there doing something that can position you to return to work is time well spent. Further, you never know what might happen that could force you to return to work more quickly than you had planned, such as a spouse that becomes disabled or a divorce that leaves you on your own. Finding work, particularly family-friendly work, under such stress may prove extremely challenging. Therefore, you must make plans now to stay marketable.

Resources

Books

Comeback Moms: How to leave work, raise children, and restart your career even if you haven't had a job in years by Monica Samuels and J.C. Conklin (Morgan Road Books, 2006).

Going Back to Work: A survival guide for comeback moms by Mary Quiqley and Loretta Kaufman (St. Martin's Griffin, 2004).

If You've Raised Kids You Can Manage Anything: Leadership Begins at Home by Anne Crittenden (Gotham Books, 2004).

Websites

Mothers and More: *www.mothersandmore.org*
A national network that provides support to mothers altering their participation in the paid workplace over the course of their active parenting years.

Rebel Dad: *www.rebeldad.com*
Provides news and information about at-home dads.

Slowlane.com: *www.slowlane.com*
An online reference, resource, and network for Stay At Home Dads and their families.

Mom's Resumes: *www.momsresumes.com*
Resume writing help and resources for moms returning to the workforce.

Bibliography

Blades, J. and K.R. Rowe-Finkbeiner. The *Motherhood Manifesto: What America's Moms Want—and What to Do About It.* New York: Nation Books, 2006.

Berger, L. *The Savvy Part-Time Professional: How to Land, Create, or Negotiate the Part-Time Job of Your Dreams.* Richmond, Va.: Capital Books, 2006.

Bouris, K. *Just Kiss Me and Tell Me You Did the Laundry: How to Negotiate Equal Roles for Husband and Wife in Parenting, Career, and Home Life.* New York: Rodale, 2004.

Carter, J. and J.D. Carter. *He Works, She Works: Successful Strategies for Working Couples.* American Management Association, New York: Random House, 1995.

Crittenden, A. *If You've Raised Kids You Can Manage Anything: Leadership Begins at Home.* New York: Gotham Books, 2004.

Crittenden, A. *The Price of Motherhood: Why the Most Important Job in the World Is Still the Least Valued.* New York: Metropolitan Books, 2001.

Dynerman, S.B. and L.O. Hayes. *The Best Jobs in America for Parents Who Want Careers and Time for Children Too.* New York: Rawson Associates, 1991.

Evans, C. *This Is How We Do It: The Working Mothers' Manifesto.* New York: Hudson Street Press, 2006.

Fisher, R., W. Ury, and B. Patton. *Getting to Yes.* New York: Random House, 2003.

Foley, J. *Flex-Time: A Working Mother's Guide to Balancing Career and Family.* New York: Marlowe & Company, 2003.

Friedman, S.D. and J.H. Greenhause. *Work and Family—Allies or Enemies?* New York: Oxford University Press, 2003.

Gill, L. *Stay-At-Home Dads: The Essential Guide to Creating the New Family.* New York: Plume Books, 2000.

Golant, M. and S. Golant. *Finding Time for Fathering: How Fathers Can Share More of Their Lives With Their Children—In Work, Chores, and Play.* New York: Fawcett-Columbine, 1992.

Henninghausen, L. *Shades of Gray: A Mother's Guide to Work and Family Choices.* Minneapolis, Minn.: Beaver's Pond Press, 2001.

Hewlett, S.A. *Creating a Life: Professional Women and the Quest for Children.* New York: Talk Miramax Books, 2002.

Johnson, T., R.F. Spizman, and L. Pollak. *Women for Hire: The Ultimate Guide to Getting a Job.* New York: Perigee, 2002.

Laqueur, M. and D. Dickinson. *Breaking Out of 9 to 5: How to Redesign Your Job to Fit You.* Princeton, N.J.: Peterson's, 1994.

Levine, J.A. and T.L. Pittinsky. *Working Fathers: New Strategies for Balancing Work and Family.* San Diego, Calif.: Harcourt Brace and Company, 1997.

Levine, S.B. *Father Courage: What Happens When Men Put Family First.* New York: Harcourt, 2000.

Mason, L. *The Working Mother's Guide to Life: Strategies, Secrets, and Solutions.* New York: Three Rivers Press, 2002.

Mockler, N. L. Young. *The End of Work as We Know It: The Common Sense Guide to America's Workplace Revolution.* Lincoln, Nebr.: Writer's Club Press, 2002.

Orenstein, P. *Flux: Women on Sex, Work, Love, Kids, and Life in a Half-Changed World.* New York: Random House, 2000.

Park, R.D. and A.A. Brott. *Throwaway Dads: The Myths and Barriers That Keep Men From Being the Fathers They Want to Be.* New York: Houghton Mifflin Company, 2003.

Quiqley, M.W. and L.E. Kaufman. *Going Back to Work: A Survival Guide For Comeback Moms.* New York: St. Martin's Griffin, 2004.

Sachs, W. *How She Really Does It: Secrets of Successful Stay-At-Work Moms.* New York: Da Capo Press, 2005.

Samuels, M. and J.C. Conklin. *Comeback Moms: How to Leave Work, Raise Children, and Restart Your Career Even If You Haven't Had a Job in Years.* New York: Morgan Road Books, 2006.

Warner, J. *Perfect Madness: Motherhood in the Age of Anxiety.* New York: Riverhead Books, New York.

Wilcox, E. *The Mom Economy: The Mothers' Guide to Getting Family Friendly Work.* New York: Berkley Books, 2003.

Zappert, L.T. *Getting It Right: How Working Mothers Successfully Take Up the Challenge of Life, Family, and Career.* New York: Pocket Books, 2001.

Index

■■

About the Author

Lori K. Long, Ph.D., SPHR, is the president of LK Consulting, LLC, a human resource management consulting firm specializing in start-up and small businesses. She holds a Ph.D. in Business Administration from Kent State University and has more than 15 years of experience in human resource management, career counseling, and business consulting. Lori is the former associate director of the Career Management Center at the Weatherhead School of Management, Case Western Reserve University, a past president of the Cleveland Society for Human Resource Management, and is certified as a senior professional in human resources. Lori's research interests include effective work/life management strategies, the policy implications of federal employment laws and regulations, and the use of technology in human resource management. She has published several articles and presented numerous seminars on these and other human resource management topics. In addition to her work with LK Consulting, Lori is an adjunct faculty member at Baldwin-Wallace College. She lives with her husband David and their two children in Cleveland, Ohio.